NASA'S ELEMENTARY AND SECONDARY EDUCATION PROGRAM

Review and Critique

Committee for the Review and Evaluation of
NASA's Precollege Education Program

Helen R. Quinn, Heidi A. Schweingruber,
and Michael A. Feder, *Editors*

Board on Science Education
Center for Education

Division of Behavioral and Social Sciences and Education

NATIONAL RESEARCH COUNCIL
OF THE NATIONAL ACADEMIES

THE NATIONAL ACADEMIES PRESS
Washington, D.C.
www.nap.edu

THE NATIONAL ACADEMIES PRESS 500 Fifth Street, N.W. Washington, DC 20001

NOTICE: The project that is the subject of this report was approved by the Governing Board of the National Research Council, whose members are drawn from the councils of the National Academy of Sciences, the National Academy of Engineering, and the Institute of Medicine. The members of the committee responsible for the report were chosen for their special competences and with regard for appropriate balance.

This study was supported by Contract No. NNH05CC15C between the National Academy of Sciences and the National Aeronautics and Space Administration (NASA). Any opinions, findings, conclusions, or recommendations expressed in this publication are those of the authors(s) and do not necessarily reflect the views of the organizations or agencies that provided support for the project.

International Standard Book Number-13: 978-0-309-11551-3
International Standard Book Number-10: 0-309-11551-5

Additional copies of this report are available from National Academies Press, 500 Fifth Street, N.W., Lockbox 285, Washington, DC 20055; (800) 624-6242 or (202) 334-3313 (in the Washington metropolitan area); Internet, http://www.nap.edu.

Suggested citation: National Research Council. (2008). *NASA's Elementary and Secondary Education Program: Review and Critique.* Committee for the Review and Evaluation of NASA's Precollege Education Program, Helen R. Quinn, Heidi A. Schweingruber, and Michael A. Feder, Editors. Board on Science Education, Center for Education. Division of Behavioral and Social Sciences and Education. Washington, DC: The National Academies Press.

THE NATIONAL ACADEMIES
Advisers to the Nation on Science, Engineering, and Medicine

The **National Academy of Sciences** is a private, nonprofit, self-perpetuating society of distinguished scholars engaged in scientific and engineering research, dedicated to the furtherance of science and technology and to their use for the general welfare. Upon the authority of the charter granted to it by the Congress in 1863, the Academy has a mandate that requires it to advise the federal government on scientific and technical matters. Dr. Ralph J. Cicerone is president of the National Academy of Sciences.

The **National Academy of Engineering** was established in 1964, under the charter of the National Academy of Sciences, as a parallel organization of outstanding engineers. It is autonomous in its administration and in the selection of its members, sharing with the National Academy of Sciences the responsibility for advising the federal government. The National Academy of Engineering also sponsors engineering programs aimed at meeting national needs, encourages education and research, and recognizes the superior achievements of engineers. Dr. Charles M. Vest is president of the National Academy of Engineering.

The **Institute of Medicine** was established in 1970 by the National Academy of Sciences to secure the services of eminent members of appropriate professions in the examination of policy matters pertaining to the health of the public. The Institute acts under the responsibility given to the National Academy of Sciences by its congressional charter to be an adviser to the federal government and, upon its own initiative, to identify issues of medical care, research, and education. Dr. Harvey V. Fineberg is president of the Institute of Medicine.

The **National Research Council** was organized by the National Academy of Sciences in 1916 to associate the broad community of science and technology with the Academy's purposes of furthering knowledge and advising the federal government. Functioning in accordance with general policies determined by the Academy, the Council has become the principal operating agency of both the National Academy of Sciences and the National Academy of Engineering in providing services to the government, the public, and the scientific and engineering communities. The Council is administered jointly by both Academies and the Institute of Medicine. Dr. Ralph J. Cicerone and Dr. Charles M. Vest are chair and vice chair, respectively, of the National Research Council.

www.national-academies.org

COMMITTEE FOR THE REVIEW AND EVALUATION OF NASA'S PRECOLLEGE EDUCATION PROGRAM

HELEN R. QUINN *(Chair)*, Stanford Linear Accelerator Center, Stanford University
EDWARD F. CRAWLEY, Department of Aeronautics and Astronautics, Massachusetts Institute of Technology
ERNEST R. HOUSE, School of Education, University of Colorado, Boulder
HARRIETT G. JENKINS, Consultant, Bethesda, MD
BRETT D. MOULDING, Utah Office of Education, Salt Lake City
BRUCE PARTRIDGE, Department of Physics and Astronomy, Haverford College
SENTA RAIZEN, WestEd, Arlington, VA
PHILIP J. SAKIMOTO, Department of Physics, University of Notre Dame
ELIZABETH K. STAGE, Lawrence Hall of Science, University of California, Berkeley
JAMES S. TREFIL, Department of Physics and Astronomy, George Mason University
CAROL H. WEISS, Harvard Graduate School of Education, Harvard University

HEIDI A. SCHWEINGRUBER, *Study Director and Acting Board Director*
MICHAEL A. FEDER, *Program Officer*
C. JEAN MOON, *Director, Board on Science Education* (until October 2007)
PATRICIA SANTOS, *Senior Program Assistant*

Foreword

The role of federal agencies in education is a critical one, but one deserving of a greater knowledge base to define and strengthen that role. This National Research Council report on the National Aeronautics and Space Administration (NASA) precollege education program that was overseen by the Board on Science Education (BOSE) makes a solid contribution to increasing this knowledge base. Public outreach and science education have been important components of the mission of NASA since the Space Act created NASA in 1958. The timing of the Space Act was clearly not an historical accident. It came in response to a successful launch of the Soviet Union's Sputnik satellite in October 1957.

The world's first artificial satellite was about the size of a basketball, weighted only 183 pounds, and took about 98 minutes to orbit the Earth on its elliptical path. That launch reflected major new political, military, technological, and scientific developments and brought attention and anxiety to U.S. readiness to match—and overtake—the Soviet Union's accomplishments.

Today, more than 50 years later, the United States is again attentive and anxious about the nation's readiness, particularly in technology and science. This review of NASA's K-12 education program comes at a time when the state of science, technology, engineering, and mathematics (STEM) education in the United States is also a focus of concerns. Those concerns range from a waning of interest among youth in STEM careers, to the quality of teacher preparation programs to ready future teachers to engage students in the ideas and practices of science and mathematics, to the growing gap between how science is practiced and how students experience the ideas of science inside and outside of the classroom. Outside of formal schooling, there is also concern about public understanding and interest in science.

Today, the state of science knowledge in our society cannot rest with only K-12 schools. More realistically, it has to be a central societal concern to all—from governmental institutions to state agencies to corporations and businesses to individual citizens. Much of everyday experience is shaped by or is a by-product of the enterprise of science, engineering, mathematics, and technologies. People's health, the health of the world's oceans and air, and the remarkable infrastructure of communications technologies are but a small percentage of everyone's everyday encounter with the productive and powerful engine of science.

Our ability to maintain this progression of invention, knowledge creation, and innovation depends upon a similar ability to interest, motivate, and educate the next generation of individuals who will successfully contribute to all facets of our country's STEM enterprise. A federal agency like NASA has a unique and important role to play in motivating and inspiring students to consider STEM careers, and citizens to become more knowledgeable participants in the scientific arena.

In a September 1962 address at Rice University, President John Kennedy spoke of the challenges to a society that he called on to undertake a great challenge: putting a man on the moon within a decade. He said

> We choose to go to the moon. We choose to go to the moon in this decade and do the other things, not because they are easy, but because they are hard, because that goal will serve to organize and measure the best of our energies and skills, because that challenge is one that we are willing to accept, one we are unwilling to postpone, and one which we intend to win, and the others, too.

These remain inspiring words—words worth remembering as we contemplate the current and future state of STEM education in this country.

BOSE is pleased to have overseen this study. Our mission is to be responsive to Congress when they request studies, but also to be responsive to the citizens of this country and their need for objective and evidence-based findings about all aspects of science education. We anticipate this report will be of genuine assistance to Congress, to NASA, and to the many other federal agencies with a commitment to STEM education.

Carl E. Wieman, *Chair*
C. Jean Moon, *Director*
Board on Science Education

Acknowledgments

The committee and staff thank the many individuals and organizations without whom this study could not have been completed. We also recognize and honor the memory of William Bryant Williams, project manager for the Aerospace Education Services Project (AESP) at the National Aeronautics and Space Administration (NASA) who presented to the committee during its deliberations. Bill was a dedicated educator with a long career in teaching and administration who made many contributions to NASA education during his tenure with the agency.

First, we acknowledge the support of NASA staff in the Office of Education who provided detailed information about NASA's activities in K-12 education. They made themselves readily available to National Research Council (NRC) staff and the committee. They were quick to respond to requests for information, contacted other NASA staff to help field requests, and were persistent in obtaining the information requested by the committee. Malcom Phelps, associate director and Shelley Canright, acting director of elementary and secondary education were especially helpful.

Individually and collectively, members of the committee benefited from discussions and presentations by those who participated in our three fact-finding meetings. NASA staff from the headquarters Office of Education, and staff and researchers associated with centers and individual projects were invaluable in providing information about the Elementary and Secondary Program and its constituent projects. We are grateful to each of the presenters: Joyce Winterton, assistant administrator for education; Shelley Canright, acting director of elementary and secondary education; Malcom Phelps, associate director; Bernice Alston, deputy assistant administrator;

James Manning, head of the office of public outreach, Space Telescope Science Institute; Isabel Hawkins, senior fellow and director of the Space Sciences Laboratory, Center for Science Education, University of California, Berkeley; Robert Gabrys, chief education officer, NASA Goddard Space Flight Center; Edna DeVore, director of education and public outreach, SETI Institute; William Bryant Williams, project manager for AESP; Edward Pritchard, project manager for Education Flight Projects (EFP); Cynthia McArthur, project manager for flight projects; Dovie Lacy, project manager for Science, Engineering, Mathematics and Aerospace Academy (SEMAA); Robert Starr, project manager, Digital Learning Network (DLN); Robert LaSalvia, project manager, NASA Explorer Schools (NES).

The committee also benefitted from presentations by experts knowledgeable about the agency, or those who had served as outside evaluators for NASA's education programs. Thanks to: Joy Frechtling, vice president, Westat; Theresa Schwerin, associate director for education, Institute for Global Environmental Strategies; Susan Cohen, director, Program Evaluation and Research Group, Lesley University; Hilarie Davis, evaluator, Technology for Learning Consortium, Inc.; Jeffrey Rosendhal, consultant; Kevin McKinley, independent evaluator.

A panel of representatives from other federal science agencies engaged in K-12 education activities provided valuable insight into the federal context for NASA's programs: Marlene Kaplan, deputy director of education, National Oceanic and Atmospheric Administration (NOAA); Bruce Fuchs, office of science education, National Institutes of Health (NIH); William Valdez, acting director of the office of workforce development and director of planning and analysis, U.S. Department of Energy (DOE); Jill Karsten, program director for diversity and education, directorate for geosciences, National Science Foundation (NSF).

Finally, the committee benefitted from the contributions of three authors of commissioned papers whose work informed this report. Frances Lawrenz, associate vice president for research at the University of Minnesota, reviewed several external evaluations of K-12 education projects in NASA and wrote a summary and critique. Susan Mundry, associate director at WestEd, provided a detailed discussion of the NASA Explorer Schools model in comparison with frameworks drawn from the literature on comprehensive school reform. Georgia Hall, on behalf of Wellesley College, and senior research scientist of the National Institute on Out-of-School Time, used a review of the literature on supporting underrepresented minority students in the sciences to develop criteria with which to critique the proposed model for the Interdisciplinary National Science Project Incorporating Research and Education Experience (INSPIRE).

Several individuals at the NRC assisted the committee. Jean Moon and Patricia Morison offered valuable suggestions at each committee meeting, as well as providing helpful comments on drafts of the report. The Space Studies Board and its director, Marcia Smith, provided insightful guidance during the committee selection and fact-finding stages of the study. Matt Von Hendy provided invaluable help with library research. We thank Kirsten Sampson Snyder, who shepherded the report through the NRC review process, Eugenia Grohman, who edited the draft report, and Yvonne Wise for processing the report through final production. We are grateful to Kemi Yai, who arranged logistics for the first and second committee meetings. Finally, we thank Patricia Santos for her able assistance in supporting the committee at every stage in its deliberations and in preparing numerous drafts and revisions of the report.

This report has been reviewed in draft form by individuals chosen for their diverse perspectives and technical expertise, in accordance with procedures approved by the NRC's Report Review Committee. The purpose of this independent review is to provide candid and critical comments that will assist the institution in making its published report as sound as possible and to ensure that the report meets institutional standards for objectivity, evidence, and responsiveness to the study charge. The review comments and draft manuscript remain confidential to protect the integrity of the deliberative process. We thank the following individuals for their review of this report: Alice M. Agogino, Department of Mechanical Engineering, University of California, Berkeley; Katy Garmany, National Optical Astronomy Observatory, Tucson, AZ; Joan Herman, National Center for Research on Evaluation, Standards and Student Testing, University of California, Los Angeles; Shelley A. Lee, Science Education, Wisconsin Department of Public Instruction, Madison, WI; Richard A. McCray, Department of Astrophysics, University of Colorado, Boulder; George D. Nelson, Department of Physics and Astronomy, Western Washington University; Barbara Olds, Liberal Arts and International Studies and McBride Honors Program, Colorado School of Mines, Golden, CO; Janet Powell, Executive Director's Office, Biological Sciences Curriculum Study, Colorado Springs, CO; and Robert Semper, Center for Learning and Teaching, The Exploratorium, San Francisco, CA.

Although the reviewers listed above provided many constructive comments and suggestions, they were not asked to endorse the content of the report nor did they see the final draft of the report before its release. Michael E. Martinez, Department of Education, University of California, Irvine, and W. Carl Lineberger, Department of Chemistry, University of Colorado, Boulder, oversaw the review of this report. Appointed by the NRC, they were responsible for making certain that an independent examination of this report was carried out in accordance with institutional procedures and that all review comments were carefully considered. Responsibility for the final content of this report rests entirely with the authors and the institution.

Contents

Executive Summary   1

1   Introduction   11

2   NASA's Education Programs   21

3   The Federal Context for Education   44

4   Analysis of NASA's K-12 Education Portfolio   57

5   Program Evaluation   90

6   Conclusions and Recommendations   112

References   132

Appendixes

A   Biographical Sketches of Committee Members and Staff   139

B   Acronyms   145

List of Tables, Figures, and Boxes

TABLES

2-1 NASA Education Portfolio Activity Categories, 36
2-2 Office of Education Funding by Program and Project for Fiscal
     2003–2008, 38
3-1 K-12 STEM Education Program Funding by Agency, 47
4-1 Objectives for Seven Core Education Programs, 82
5-1 Descriptions of Reports from External Evaluations of the Core
     Projects, 92
5-2 Objectives, Outputs, and Outcomes for the Elementary and
     Secondary Program, 100

FIGURES

2-1 NASA organizational chart, 30
2-2 NASA education strategic coordination framework pyramid showing
     outcomes mapped to the education strategic framework, 32
2-3 NASA education strategic coordination framework, 33

BOXES

1-1   Programs and Projects: Definitions, 14
2-1   NASA Education Program: History of Key Changes, 23
4-1   Goals and Intended Outcomes: NASA Core K-12 Education
      Projects, 64
4-2   Examples of High-Quality NASA Partnership Projects in
      Education, 85

Executive Summary

The federal role in precollege science, technology, engineering, and mathematics (STEM) education is receiving increasing attention in light of the need to support public understanding of science and to develop a strong scientific and technical workforce in a competitive global economy. Federal science agencies, such as the National Aeronautics and Space Administration (NASA), are being looked to as a resource for enhancing precollege STEM education and bringing more young people to scientific and technical careers.

For NASA and other federal science agencies, concerns about workforce and public understanding of science also have an immediate local dimension. The agency faces an aerospace workforce skewed toward those close to retirement and job recruitment competition for those with science and engineering degrees. In addition, public support for the agency's missions stems in part from public understanding of the importance of the agency's contributions in science, engineering, and space exploration.

COMMITTEE TASK

In the NASA authorization act of 2005 (P.L. 109-555 Subtitle B-Education, Sec. 614) Congress directed the agency to support a review and evaluation of its precollege education program to be carried out by the National Research Council (NRC). The legislation mandated that the review include recommendations to improve the effectiveness of the program and address four tasks:

1. an evaluation of the effectiveness of the overall program in meeting its defined goals and objectives;
2. an assessment of the quality and educational effectiveness of the major components of the program, including an evaluation of the adequacy of assessment metrics and data collection requirements available for determining the effectiveness of individual projects;
3. an evaluation of the funding priorities in the program, including a review of the funding level and trend for each major component of the program and an assessment of whether the resources made available are consistent with meeting identified goals and priorities; and
4. a determination of the extent and effectiveness of coordination and collaboration between NASA and other federal agencies that sponsor science, technology, and mathematics education activities.

NASA, in consultation with the NRC, interpreted the charge to mean a focus on the Elementary and Secondary Program managed by the Office of Education. This program includes seven projects:

1. the Aerospace Education Services Project (AESP)
2. the Science, Engineering, Mathematics and Aerospace Academy (SEMAA)
3. NASA Explorer Schools (NES)
4. the Digital Learning Network (DLN)
5. Education Flight Projects (EFP)
6. the Educator Astronaut Project (EAP)
7. the Interdisciplinary National Science Project Incorporating Research and Education Experience (INSPIRE)

The study committee reviewed a wide range of documents related to NASA's programs in precollege STEM education, heard testimony from NASA staff, and commissioned three papers. As is the case with many federal science agencies involved in education outreach, only a limited number of external evaluations of NASA education projects have been conducted. As a consequence, the committee also relied on relevant research evidence and committee members' collective expertise when drawing conclusions about how projects could be improved. The committee developed specific recommendations for only three of the seven projects—NES, AESP, and SEMAA—because the other four projects had been in place too short a time or lacked sufficient documentation of project performance.

The report provides a summary of the committee's findings regarding the recent history of NASA's education program and K-12 projects (Chapter 2) and the federal context for NASA's role in K-12 education, including discussion of other science agencies (Chapter 3). It also discusses each of the seven projects in depth with specific suggestions for improvement (Chapter 4). Finally, it reviews NASA's current approach to project review and evaluation and offers suggestions for improving the process (Chapter 5). Chapter 6 of the report details the committee's conclusions and recommendations.

CONTEXT OF K-12 EDUCATION AT NASA

Education and contributing to public understanding of science have been important components of NASA's mission since its creation by the 1958 Space Act. NASA does not, however, have the lead federal role in pre-college STEM education, which is the responsibility of the National Science Foundation and the U.S. Department of Education. Rather, as a discoverer of new science and a creator of new technology, NASA, like other federal science agencies, has an important complementary role in STEM education. That role is closely linked to and guided by the core scientific, engineering, and exploration missions of the agency.

The bulk of the K-12 STEM education activities in the agency are in the Office of Education and the Science Mission Directorate (SMD), which each account for about 50 percent of the agency's total funding for K-12 STEM education. Thus, the seven projects that make up the Elementary and Secondary Program in the headquarters Office of Education on which this review was to focus represent only about one-half of the activities in K-12 education undertaken by the agency.

Traditionally, the Office of Education and SMD have had different approaches to developing and implementing K-12 education projects. SMD devotes a percentage of funds connected with each major science mission to education activities. Proposed education activities connected to each mission are described as part of the proposal for science funding and undergo competitive expert review. In contrast, the Office of Education is supported by a line item in NASA's budget. Projects are developed by Office of Education staff or originate in NASA field centers and are then expanded. This history has resulted in a broad and diverse portfolio of projects that vary in scope, target audiences, and objectives. In 2006 the agency adopted a new strategic coordination framework that is designed to bring coherence to the education activities across the agency; it was in the early stages of implementation as the committee's study was done.

CONCLUSIONS

The committee's conclusions regarding the effectiveness of NASA's K-12 education program and areas for improvement are summarized here as responses to the four purposes stated by congress. Given the charge to the committee from Congress and from NASA, the committee focused on the seven specified core programs. The committee also took a wider view of NASA's entire portfolio in K-12 STEM education in drawing its conclusions.

Effectiveness of the Elementary and Secondary Program

The committee was limited in its ability to draw conclusions about the overall effectiveness of the headquarters Office of Education's Elementary and Secondary Program because of instability in the program and lack of rigorous evaluation. NASA's education portfolio has experienced rapidly shifting priorities, fluctuations in budget, and changes in management structure that have undermined the stability of programs and made evaluation of effectiveness challenging.

NASA does not have a coherent overall plan for evaluation and for how results of evaluation should inform program and project design and implementation. Few of NASA's projects have been formally evaluated, and none has been evaluated rigorously. Consequently, there are little data across projects on which to base conclusions about effectiveness.

Effectiveness of Individual Projects and Adequacy of Assessment Metrics

The Elementary and Secondary Program overall is to be commended for its effort to reach underrepresented groups. The committee concludes that the seven specified core projects are somewhat effective at raising awareness of the science and engineering of NASA's missions and generating students' and teachers' interest in STEM subjects. As currently configured, however, the projects cannot be shown to be effective at enhancing learning of STEM content or providing in-depth experiences with the science and engineering of the missions.

Evaluation of individual projects is complicated by the fact that individual projects have taken on the broad goals of the Elementary and Secondary Program rather than developing project-specific, focused goals and objectives that are appropriate to the design and scope of individual projects. Currently, data collection efforts common to all projects chiefly consist of counts of sessions offered, numbers of participants, and immediate feedback from them. Such data are insufficient to evaluate the effectiveness of projects or of the program as a whole. The current data collection system, the NASA Education Evaluation Information System (NEEIS), is inadequate for supporting effective evaluation and has technical shortcomings.

Funding Priorities

NASA has demonstrated a strong commitment to funding STEM education activities. However, because K-12 activities originate in different administrative units in the agency, it is difficult to track all of the funding for K-12 education. Funding for education through the Office of Education has declined from $230 million in 2003 to $153 million in 2007 and has been significantly affected by an increasing number of congressionally directed appropriations (CDAs, also known as earmarks). Such fluctuations in budget have undermined the program's stability and coherence.

NASA does not appear to have budgeted sufficient funds for a thorough evaluation of projects; however, because budgets for evaluation are reported as project costs, information on total funds targeted specifically for evaluations is unavailable. The committee questions whether the agency has sufficient resources and expertise to adequately support the school-level curricular reform efforts of the NASA Explorer Schools project. NASA should also consider whether current information and communications technology could be used to improve the cost-effectiveness of some projects.

Coordination and Collaboration Between NASA and Other Federal Agencies

NASA has participated in federally coordinated activities, but NASA does not systematically coordinate with other federal agencies involved in STEM education nor interact with other federal agencies to draw on expertise related to the design of STEM education projects. There have been a limited number of cross-agency projects in which NASA has had good collaboration with other federal agencies such as the GLOBE program, which is sponsored by NASA, the National Science Foundation, and the Department of State with cooperation from many organizations and government agencies including the National Oceanic and Atmospheric Administration and the Department of Education.

RECOMMENDATIONS

The committee identified four broad areas that are important for improving NASA's efforts in K-12 STEM education: (1) the nature of NASA's role in K-12 STEM education, (2) continuous improvement of projects, (3) partnerships and expertise in education, and (4) information and communications technology. Additional, detailed recommendations for individual projects are included in Chapter 6 (the numbering here follows that used in the chapter).

NASA's Role in K-12 STEM Education

Recommendation 1   NASA should continue to engage in education activities at the K-12 level, designing its K-12 education activities so that they capitalize on NASA's primary strengths and resources, which are found in the mission directorates. These strengths and resources are the agency's scientific discoveries; its technology and aeronautical developments; its space exploration activities; the scientists, engineers, and other technical staff (both internal and external) who carry out NASA's work; and the unique excitement generated by space flight and space exploration.

Recommendation 2   The exciting nature of NASA's mission gives particular value to projects whose primary goal is to inspire and engage students' interest in science and engineering, and NASA's education portfolio should include projects with these goals. Because engineering and technology development are subjects that are not well covered in K-12 curricula, projects aimed at inspiring and engaging students in these areas are particularly important.

Recommendation 3   NASA should provide opportunities for teachers and students to deepen their knowledge about NASA-supported areas of science and the nature of science and engineering through educational activities that engage them with the science and engineering carried out by the mission directorates.

Recommendation 4   NASA should strive to support stability in its education programs, in terms of funding, management structure, and priorities.

Recommendation 8   The NASA headquarters Office of Education should focus on leadership and advocacy for inclusion of education activities in the programs of NASA's four operating directorates, quality assurance, internal coordination, and coordination with other agencies and organizations. In the development of new education projects, the office should partner closely with the directorates or centers and consult with external education experts.

Continuous Project Improvement

NASA has not adopted mechanisms to ensure continuous improvement of projects within the Elementary and Secondary Program. For example, goals and objectives for individual projects reflect very closely the overall goals for the entire elementary and secondary program and are not well calibrated to the scope and target audience of individual projects. Effective program design and management requires that a project's goals, desired outcomes, and evaluation metrics be aligned. This alignment is not generally the case for the seven Office of Education precollege projects that this committee was asked to examine.

NASA also lacks an overall plan for evaluation of its precollege portfolio and projects. Such a plan should include definition of measurable project goals and objectives, framing of the purposes of evaluations and key questions, and a plan for how information from the evaluation will inform the design and implementation of projects. NASA's new strategic coordination framework for education is designed to address these issues of review and evaluation; however, it is still in initial stages of implementation.

Recommendation 5   NASA should take a more intentional approach to portfolio development than it has to date so that individual projects are well defined and have clear and realistic goals and objectives given their target audiences. Management of the resulting portfolio should include periodic review of the balance of investment across projects.

Recommendation 17   NASA should develop an overall evaluation plan for its K-12 education program and projects and allocate the resources needed to implement the plan.

Recommendation 18   For portfolio management, the NASA evaluation plan should include some cross-project evaluations as well as project-specific evaluations.

Recommendation 19   NASA should plan the scale, design, and frequency of each project evaluation so that it aligns to the scale and goals of the project, and to the nature of the decisions that need to be made.

Recommendation 20   NASA should use evaluation findings to inform project design as well as project improvement. To do so, NASA should establish mechanisms to connect evaluations to program and project decisions.

Partnerships and Expertise in Education

Given NASA's primary focus on science, engineering, and technology, the agency employs a large staff with expertise in these areas. The number of agency staff who have primary expertise in education is limited. The technical staff in the agency cannot be expected to have sufficient expertise in K-12 STEM education to allow them to develop effective education projects on their own. Thus, the scientists and engineers in the agency need to work in concert with experts in education, often from outside the agency, in order to achieve the appropriate mix of expertise in science, engineering and education to design and implement effective education projects.

Recommendation 6   NASA program and project planning and execution should make better and more consistent use of opportunities to involve education stakeholders, to partner with individuals and organizations that can provide expertise in education, and to connect to the existing infrastructure for K-12 STEM education.

Recommendation 7   NASA's partnerships in education should be designed in light of the specific objectives of each project. NASA can play a lead role in projects intended to inspire and engage students and should use strategic partnerships to leverage the impact of such projects. For projects designed to affect schools through work with students, teachers, or curriculum materials, NASA should work in partnerships with organizations that complement NASA's science and engineering expertise with education-specific expertise and avenues of dissemination. All partnerships should begin during the early stages of project design.

Information and Communications Technology

The agency's K-12 education projects do not appear to be using information and communications technology effectively. Projects tend to use technology that was modern at the time of inception and do not make efforts to periodically update it. Continued use of the outdated information and communications technology can lead to inefficiencies in the use of project funds.

Recommendation 9   NASA should make better use of current and emerging information and communications technology to provide broader and more user-friendly access to NASA materials, to support

NASA's K-12 STEM education activities, to extend the reach of NASA's education activities, and to maintain a centralized data system.

Recommendation 10 NASA should periodically review each project to determine whether its components are the most cost-effective uses of resources, given current information and communications technology alternatives.

Overall, NASA makes significant contributions to K-12 education by providing access to its expertise in science, engineering, technology, and space exploration. It is uniquely positioned to inspire and engage students in STEM subjects and to expose teachers and students to the nature of science and engineering through exposure to the agency's missions. However, the Elementary and Secondary Program is not realizing NASA's potential as a resource for education as effectively as could be hoped. Developing a culture of ongoing improvement, cultivating sustained partnerships that bring in expertise in education, and using information and communication technology more effectively are promising strategies for improving NASA's programs in K-12 education. When these are linked to a coherent and well-funded plan for evaluation, the agency stands poised to have a positive and demonstrable impact on learning and teaching in STEM subjects.

1

Introduction

Public outreach and science education have been important components of the mission of the National Aeronautics and Space Administration (NASA) since its creation in 1958. NASA's strategy for promoting these components has evolved during the life of the agency, and it has undergone considerable change in the last 10 years. Most recently, as part of a restructuring of the entire agency, agencywide education programs at NASA were reorganized and subjected to an internal review guided by a new, detailed strategic plan for education (National Aeronautics and Space Administration, 2006a). The reorganization and new education plan provide a unique opportunity for a review and evaluation of NASA's past and ongoing activities in education.

This report focuses on NASA's K-12 education activities, as mandated by congressional language in the 2005 reauthorizing legislation for the agency. The review comes at a time when science, technology, engineering, and mathematics (STEM) education is a subject of increasing national concern. Focus on STEM education primarily reflects a concern that national competitiveness, both economic and security related, requires that a high percentage of students leaving high school are capable and motivated to pursue careers in science and technology. It also reflects concern that there is a lack of public understanding of science and scientific inquiry. On the first point, if the United States is to remain scientifically innovative and competitive in an increasingly globalized economy, preparing students for science and engineering careers is imperative. On the second point, a democratic society needs all citizens to be scientifically literate in order to participate in national debates on such scientific issues as climate change and alternative fuels. For NASA, there is also a local issue as the agency faces an aerospace workforce that is skewed toward employees who are nearing retirement, as well as competition in recruiting job candidates with science and engineering degrees.

One response to these concerns has been to reexamine the role of federal science agencies in supporting and advancing STEM education for kindergarten through grade 12 (K-12). This study of NASA's K-12 education portfolio provides an opportunity not only to examine NASA's activities in grades K-12, but also to examine the larger issue of defining the appropriate role for science agencies in supporting improved K-12 STEM education.

THE COMMITTEE'S CHARGE AND APPROACH

The Committee to Review and Evaluate NASA's Precollege Education Portfolio was established by the National Research Council (NRC) to undertake this study. The committee included 12 members with expertise in the history and structure of NASA education programs; program evaluation for a range of program types (specifically targeted to the kinds of projects in the NASA portfolio); science and mathematics instruction at both the elementary and secondary levels, with particular knowledge of earth and space sciences; teacher professional development; education policy and practice in science and mathematics at the state and local levels; and measurement. Special emphasis was given to identifying individuals for this committee who have a working knowledge of NASA as an organization, as well as knowledge of NASA's Elementary and Secondary Education Program (see Appendix A for biographical sketches).

The study focused on the purposes identified by Congress in its charge to the study committee to "conduct a review and evaluation of NASA's precollege science, technology and mathematics education program. The review and evaluation shall include such recommendations as the NRC determines will improve the effectiveness of the program and include

1. an evaluation of the effectiveness of the overall program in meeting its defined goals and objectives;
2. an assessment of the quality and educational effectiveness of the major components of the program, including an evaluation of the adequacy of assessment metrics and data collection requirements available for determining the effectiveness of individual projects;
3. an evaluation of the funding priorities in the program, including a review of the funding level and trend for each major component of the program and an assessment of whether the resources made available are consistent with meeting identified goals and priorities; and

4. a determination of the extent and effectiveness of coordination and collaboration between NASA and other federal agencies that sponsor science, technology, and mathematics education activities.

The NASA headquarters Office of Education and the NRC agreed to focus the review on the seven projects in the Elementary and Secondary Education Program (see Box 1-1 for a definition of programs and projects).[1] Those projects are referred to in this report as the seven core projects:

1. The Aerospace Education Services Project (AESP) provides training for teachers to use NASA STEM curricula and new and evolving education pedagogy and supports student STEM education through student projects, classroom visits, and inquiry-based activities. AESP employs former teachers who travel nationwide to work with teachers, students, and schools to improve STEM education. The majority of AESP activities are in NASA Explorer Schools (see below).

2. The Science, Engineering, Mathematics and Aerospace Academy (SEMAA) is conducted during and after school for K-12 students to expose historically underrepresented youth to activities in the fields of science, engineering, mathematics, and technology. SEMAA includes three components: curricular support materials for use during and after school, interactive family activities, and access to NASA technology at Aerospace Education Laboratories.

3. The NASA Explorer Schools (NES) project immerses selected high-minority and high-poverty urban and rural middle schools in NASA mission content by providing them access to NASA resources, people, and products. It is implemented through 3-year partnerships between NASA and the selected school teams, which are identified by the NASA centers.[2]

4. The Digital Learning Network (DLN)[3] makes NASA's educational resources and its scientists and engineers available to students and teachers through video conferencing.

5. Education Flight Projects (EFP) provides a way for students and teachers to capitalize on the data and images provided by NASA's

---

[1]Projects aimed at museums and science centers fall within the Office of Education's Informal Education Program and were not included in the review.

[2]The term "centers" in this report refers to the nine NASA field centers and the Jet Propulsion Laboratory.

[3]Although the DLN was an activity within the NES when the committee began its work, there were discussions in NASA's Office of Education about making it an independent project. Therefore, NASA staff requested that we treat it as such for the purposes of our study.

BOX 1-1
Programs and Projects: Definitions

Program is a group of projects that are guided by a common set of overarching goals and share similar target audiences. The NASA Office of Education has five programs: elementary and secondary education, higher education, e-education, informal education, and the Minority University Research Education Program (MUREP).

Projects are the component parts of programs and include a set of activities that address the same specific measurable goals aimed at a specific audience. The seven projects that are the primary focus of this study make up the Elementary and Secondary Program in the Office of Education. In some cases, the formal name of a project includes the word "program": for example, the Aerospace Education Services Program. We have chosen to refer to these as projects for the sake of clarity because they are part of the Elementary and Secondary Program.

---

scientific and exploration missions and interact with astronauts on the International Space Station.

6. The Educator Astronaut Project (EAP) includes the educator astronaut recruitment and selection activities that guide the recruitment of a small number of qualified educators to join the Astronaut Corps. These teachers develop educational material related to their work as astronauts. A subset of teachers chosen through the selection process, who do not join the Astronaut Corps, are selected to form the Network of Educator Astronaut Teachers. These teachers serve as NASA education advocates by engaging their schools and communities in NASA education activities.

7. The Interdisciplinary National Science Project Incorporating Research and Education Experience (INSPIRE), which is under development, is a three-tiered project designed to maximize student participation and involvement in STEM and to enhance the STEM pipeline from middle school through high school to the undergraduate college level.

Recognizing that there are education activities related to K-12 education located outside of the Elementary and Secondary Program, the committee initially considered including all NASA projects related to K-12.

However, the preliminary information we collected confirmed that an all-inclusive and detailed review was impossible given time and budget constraints. Thus, the committee carried out its charge to focus mainly on the seven core projects with recognition that they do not capture the full range of the agency's K-12 education activities.

For comparison purposes the committee included some examination of K-12 education activities that are based in the Science Mission Directorate (SMD) and are not directly managed by the Elementary and Secondary Program However, due to the resources and timeline of the study, the examination of these activities was necessarily more limited. The SMD has been especially active in developing education projects and materials. Over the course of this review, the committee discovered that in fiscal 2006, the SMD spent about the same amount of money on K-12 STEM education projects as the headquarters Office of Education. The SMD's work is largely separate from the agencywide programs managed by the headquarters Office of Education. Thus, the committee considers the seven core projects in the context of the broader portfolio of K-12 education activities in NASA.

The committee carried out its work through an iterative process of gathering information, analyzing and deliberating it, identifying gaps and questions, gathering additional information to fill these gaps, and carrying out further analysis and deliberations. The contractually determined time and resources for the study constrained the scope of the committee's review to existing documentation and discussions with NASA program and project staff. The committee did not carry out extensive original data collection. Because of these constraints, the study is best thought of as an expert review rather than a formal program evaluation.

In its search for relevant information, the committee held three public fact-finding meetings; reviewed documents related to NASA's K-12 education portfolio, such as budget requests, project evaluations, project plans, and other technical reports; and commissioned background papers.

Over the first three meetings, the committee heard presentations and engaged in discussions with staff of the NASA Office of Education who are involved with K-12 education projects, as well as directors of education and outreach projects based in NASA's SMD. The committee members were also briefed by people who had conducted evaluations of some specific NASA education projects. At the second meeting, in addition to presentations about NASA's projects, the committee explored the larger question of how federal science agencies can best engage in K-12 education activities, through a panel discussion among representatives from the Department of Energy, the National Oceanic and Atmospheric Administration, the National Institutes of Health, and the National Science Foundation. At the third meeting, the committee heard only from NASA staff affiliated with the Elementary and Secondary Program.

The committee also commissioned three papers to provide background and in-depth analysis. One paper provided a critique of existing external evaluations of NASA's K-12 education projects. Another paper provided an analysis of the Explorer Schools Project in the context of what is known about successful models for comprehensive and subject specific school reform. The authors of these two papers presented early drafts of their work at the committee's third meeting. The third paper, commissioned after the third meeting, compared the proposed model of INSPIRE with successful models from multiyear projects focused on engaging students in science and engineering. These three papers were valuable resources for the committee in developing our conclusions and recommendations and writing this report.

OVERVIEW OF NASA'S EDUCATION PROGRAMS

NASA's K-12 STEM education projects are in the headquarters Office of Education, the mission directorates, and the centers. Some of the projects are deeply embedded in the research and exploration activities of the agency; others are more general, agency-supported projects that draw broadly on NASA's science, technology, and engineering resources. These latter projects are managed primarily in the headquarters Office of Education, which houses the Elementary and Secondary Education Program. The projects that are closely tied to the research exploration activities of the agency are managed entirely in individual mission directorates. The mission-embedded projects have a particular responsibility to inform the public about the science and engineering of each mission and to make resources available for educators who want to include this content in their teaching. Most of these projects are carried out by non-NASA employees in universities or research institutions that report to and work under the guidance of NASA mission directorate staff.

The headquarters Office of Education and mission K-12 projects tend to operate independently, although both may have staff housed in the same center that work together and share some resources and information. The educational efforts within the mission directorates and in the NASA centers collectively contribute to the agency's education goals, objectives, and outcomes. Recently, to support the agency's strategic education coordination framework, the Office of Education developed an education portfolio that aligns with the agency's strategic plan, provides a governance structure, and creates an agencywide strategic planning, implementation, and evaluation framework for education. The education portfolio is described in Chapter 2.

PREVIOUS REVIEWS OF NASA'S EDUCATION PROGRAMS

There have been two previous major efforts to review and evaluate NASA's education activities. Both reviewed the entire portfolio, including not only K-12 activities, but also higher education, informal science, and public outreach. In the early 1990s, NASA asked the NRC for advice and assistance in how to manage and monitor an expanding portfolio of education activities. The resulting NASA Education Programs Outcomes Committee was charged with defining appropriate goals for NASA's education projects and recommending data collection procedures and indicators that would show whether the projects were effectively meeting their goals.

The first committee's report (National Research Council, 1994) contained a set of recommended goals and indicators for assessing the quality of NASA's education projects, including those at the K-12 level. The committee further recommended that NASA gradually and deliberately undertake implementation of the indicator system described in its report; that NASA dedicate a fixed percentage of its education budget (5–10%) to indicators and evaluation; and that NASA continually review the agency's collection of programs.

One of the core projects for the current review, AESP, existed at the time of the 1994 review and was included in the analysis. However, its focus has changed considerably in recent years. The other projects that this committee was asked to review did not exist when the previous NRC committee conducted its review. However, the goals and indicators developed by that committee in the 1994 report may still be relevant to the current portfolio and were taken into consideration by the current committee.

In 2001, at the direction of the Office of Management and Budget, NASA contracted for an external evaluation of its education program. The purpose was to determine the extent to which the NASA education program provides an important contribution to the federal education portfolio, as well as to provide an assessment of the program's strengths and opportunities for improvement. The review focused on five questions:

1. Is there an appropriate role in education for NASA that is unique from other federal agencies such as the U.S. Department of Education and the National Science Foundation?
2. What is the appropriate role for NASA in education?
3. Has NASA established appropriate goals and objectives for its education program?
4. Is the NASA Implementation Plan a document that can effectively guide the education program to achieve the identified goals and objectives?

5. Is NASA's education program effective at achieving its established goals and objectives for the appropriate balance of recipients?

A seven-member expert panel was appointed to carry out the review. They reviewed evaluation data and other materials and participated in a 3-day session to examine NASA plans and projects. They reviewed the professional literature, existing data, strategic plans, and testimony by selected project administrators and program participants. They produced a report of their findings and recommendations for future direction (Westat, 2001). The expert panel concluded that NASA has a unique opportunity to use its facilities and personnel to enrich science education from the K-12 level through the Ph.D. degree level. They emphasized that part of NASA's role is to transfer and infuse the results of NASA research, development, and technology into the nation's STEM education efforts. They also concluded that NASA had established appropriate goals, had an appropriate implementation plan, and had been effective in reaching its goals.

PREVIOUS REVIEWS OF OTHER FEDERAL STEM EDUCATION PROGRAMS

In order to review and evaluate NASA's K-12 education portfolio, the committee determined that it needed to identify and understand the various ways that other federal science agencies are or could be involved in K-12 education. Thus, this study connects to early and ongoing efforts to assess the role of federal science agencies in STEM education, including several reports and the ongoing efforts of the Academic Competitiveness Council.

In 1993, recognizing the need to enhance the coordination of federal STEM programs, the Committee on Education and Human Resources of the Federal Coordinating Council for Science, Engineering and Technology (FCCSET) formulated a 5-year agenda. The first step was to appoint an expert panel charged with conducting a broad review of federal programs in STEM education and assessing federal program evaluation efforts. The panel developed a report that recommended improved management and coordination of programs, a more balanced distribution of existing funds, and comprehensive program evaluation (Federal Coordinating Council for Science, Engineering and Technology, 1993). The panel's findings confirmed that coordination of federal programs across agencies and governmental levels, and the private sector, was minimal. In addition, it concluded that core federal programs in STEM lack balance and coherence. The panel found that federal spending on STEM was not guided by assessments of national need, that few federal programs had been thoroughly evaluated to determine their effectiveness, and that funding for evaluation and evaluation personnel was extremely limited. Furthermore, evaluation practices were often inadequate for the purpose of improving programs, making informed decisions about program retention or expansion, and providing for accountability.

More recently, the Academic Competitiveness Council (ACC), established through the Deficit Reduction Act of 2005, was charged with reviewing all federal programs with a focus on mathematics and science education, and reporting its findings to Congress in February 2007. The ACC's goal was to ensure the greatest return from the government's investment in STEM education. As a result, the ACC's effort focused most closely on program effectiveness, overlap, and duplication.

In its report (U.S. Department of Education, 2007a), the ACC states that K-12 STEM education programs should focus on student learning, teacher quality, and student engagement. As did the FCCSET's expert panel report, the ACC report concluded that nearly all of the reviewed federal programs lacked rigorous metrics and methods for evaluation. The ACC recommended

> [T]he ACC program inventory, goals, and metrics should be a living resource updated regularly; agencies and the federal government should foster knowledge of effective practices through improved evaluation and/or implementation of proven-effective, research based instructional materials and methods; Federal agencies should improve their coordination of K-12 STEM education programs with state and local school systems; Federal agencies should adjust program designs and operation so that programs can be assessed and measurable results can be achieved; funding for STEM education programs should not increase unless a plan for appropriately rigorous, independent evaluation is in place; Agencies with STEM education programs should collaborate on implementing the ACC recommendations under the auspices of the National Science and Technology Council. (U.S. Department of Education, 2007a, p. 34)

The ACC recommendations demonstrate that the situation today is not very different from the portrait of federal investments in STEM education painted by the FCCSET expert panel in 1993 (Federal Coordinating Council for Science, Engineering and Technology, 1993). This context of little coordination and limited rigorous evaluation presents a challenge to the present committee for addressing the first and fourth major items in its charge, "[to make] a determination of the effectiveness of the overall program in meeting its defined goals and objectives; [to make] a determination of the extent and effectiveness of coordination and collaboration between NASA and other Federal agencies that sponsor science, technology, and mathematics education activities."

Thus, the committee determined that a critical step in assessing NASA's K-12 activities was to identify the appropriate roles for a federal science and technology agency in STEM education and then to articulate the unique contributions that NASA can and should make.

ORGANIZATION OF THE REPORT

This report reviews NASA's K-12 STEM education projects. It specifically focuses on the purposes identified by Congress in its mandate to the study committee. Furthermore, it provides guidance to NASA's continued efforts to support K-12 STEM education. This chapter introduces the goals and scope of the study, and previous efforts to review NASA's and all federal agencies' K-12 STEM education projects.

Chapter 2 provides an overview of NASA's K-12 STEM education program, a historical account of NASA's involvement in this area, and a description of NASA's K-12 framework for education projects within the headquarters Office of Education, the mission directorates, and the centers.

Chapter 3 illustrates the role of the federal government and federal agencies in K-12 STEM education. It specifically outlines the role of federal science agencies, and NASA in particular.

Chapter 4 evaluates the NASA portfolio in K-12 STEM education based on briefings from NASA staff, administrative documents, annual reports, recent external evaluations, and research in K-12 education regarding best practices in professional development, curriculum, instruction, and school reform. Particular attention was paid to program design and effectiveness in regard to the seven core Office of Education projects.

Chapter 5 critiques NASA's previous project evaluations and provides a framework for guiding future project evaluations.

Chapter 6 presents conclusions and recommendations. Based on these conclusions and recommendations, the report specifically answers the four congressionally mandated questions described earlier in this chapter.

2

NASA's Education Programs

As noted in Chapter 1, NASA has a long history of education programs, dating back to its authorization in 1958. The original authorizing legislation gives the agency responsibility for effectively sharing knowledge of the atmosphere and space with the public and ensuring that the United States remains a leader in aeronautics and space science technology. The agency's commitment to promoting science education is further supported by its responsibility as a federal agency to safeguard the public's investment in science and engineering.

NASA brings a number of unique assets to support its work in science education, including state-of-the-art facilities and awe-inspiring missions; enthusiastic and knowledgeable astronauts, scientists, and engineers; and a wealth of images, data, and scientific findings from nearly five decades of space missions. These assets are unparalleled national resources that provide students and teachers with opportunities to engage with modern science and engineering advancements, as well as the nature of scientific discovery. NASA's resources are particularly well suited to inspiring and motivating young people. Missions involving human space flight, as well as missions like the Hubble Space Telescope and Mars Exploration Rovers, have the ability to capture young people's attention in ways that are visceral and powerful (Hopkins, 2007a). These missions and resources strongly support NASA's role as a resource for the motivational and content aspects of K-12 science, technology, engineering, and mathematics (STEM) education.

This chapter provides an overview of both the recent history of NASA's education programs and its current approach to K-12 STEM education. It highlights the major endeavors developed and implemented in the agency's

Office of Education and touches on work in the science mission directorate and centers. Changes in program goals, management, and funding are also described.

For this report, recent history refers primarily to the period from the beginning of the agency's education strategy in 1992 to 2005, when a new NASA administrator began a reorganization of the education programs. The current approach covers events that occurred between 2005 and the writing of this report during the summer of 2007. It is important to note that because changes occurred while the committee was still at work it was difficult to capture a precise description of the agency's current education programs and projects.

RECENT HISTORY: 1992–2005

From the late 1970s through the early 2000s, NASA's education programs consisted of a suite of projects managed by several offices. Projects that targeted national audiences were managed by the Office of Education at NASA headquarters and implemented by the education directors at the NASA centers, who also designed and carried out a variety of regional and local projects. Projects in the Minority University Research and Education Program (MUREP) were managed by the Office of Equal Opportunity Programs at NASA headquarters, and implemented by the equal opportunity officers at the NASA centers. Some relatively independent projects were designed and implemented by NASA science and engineering organizations or their missions.

For K-12 projects, there were two main NASA units that funded and managed projects: the headquarters Office of Education and the science and technology enterprises, later renamed mission directorates.[1] The projects under each of these two main units were funded through different mechanisms and operated somewhat independently of each other. The Office of Education receives federal funding for specific projects in its portfolio, while the science and technology enterprises designate a certain level of funding from their mission or research budgets to support related education activities. Consequently, K-12 education projects across the agency tended to evolve as a diverse portfolio of often disconnected activities.

---

[1] Many of the MUREP projects also served K-12 students and teachers, but since they are implemented through grants to minority universities, they are considered by NASA to be higher education projects. MUREP activities were thus not considered to be within the scope of the agency's K-12 education projects for this study.

Defining Goals and Objectives

In 1992, in response to mandates from the Federal Coordinating Council for Science, Engineering and Technology (FCCSET) and NASA's appropriation legislation for fiscal 1992 and 1993, NASA published its first agencywide education strategy. This strategy asserted that "it is NASA's policy to use its inspiring mission, its unique facilities, and its specialized workforce to conduct and facilitate science, mathematics, engineering, and technology education programs and activities" (National Aeronautics and Space Administration, 1992, p. 5), and that the authority for this policy was derived from the agency's original legislation in 1958.

In K-12 education, the stated objective was to use NASA's mission to enhance the content, knowledge, skill, and experience of teachers; to capture the interest of students; and to channel that interest into related career paths through the demonstration of the application of science, mathematics, technology, and related subject matter. These broad goals for NASA's education programs have remained largely unchanged as NASA's education strategies have been revised.

But while the goals have remained relatively stable, there have been substantial shifts in the organization and administration of NASA's K-12 education activities. There have also been shifts in the emphasis placed on specific objectives and the strategies for achieving those objectives: Box 2-1 shows some of the changes and major milestones. These shifts complicate the task of assessing the impact of NASA's work in K-12 education activities over time.

BOX 2-1
NASA Education Program: History of Key Changes

~1962 The Aerospace Education Services Project (AESP) is established.

1992 Dan S. Golden is named administrator of NASA; the agency publishes its first agencywide education strategy.

1993 The Science, Engineering, Mathematics and Aerospace Academy (SEMAA) is established.

1994 The NASA education portfolio is reviewed by the National Research Council; a new agencywide strategic plan designates education as an agencywide goal.

1995 The first space science education strategy is published, calling for involvement of scientists in education.

continued

BOX 2-1 Continued

1996   A new agencywide strategic plan establishes education as an agency-wide contribution to its five national priorities.

       An implementation plan for space science education strategy is published; it emphasizes scientists working in high-leverage partnerships with educators.

1997   The space science education program is implemented; it requires every space science mission to use 1–2 percent of its resources on education.

1999   The NASA Implementation Plan for Education 1999–2003 is published.

2001   Sean O'Keefe is named administrator of NASA.

2002   The NASA Office of Education is elevated to "enterprise" status in the agency.

       Adena Williams Loston is named NASA's associate administrator for education.

2003   A new agencywide strategic plan focuses the education enterprise goals on inspiring and motivating students to pursue science, technology, engineering, and mathematics careers and engaging the public in the experience of exploration and discovery. The plan calls for common goals and coordination across all NASA education programs.

       The Office of Education reduces the number of education programs in its portfolio as a result of an internal review.

       The NASA Explorer Schools (NES) project (with the Digital Learning Network as a component) is established.

       The NASA Education Flight Projects is established, giving a new name and home for ongoing activities.

2004   An agencywide reorganization is implemented, as suggested by the President's Commission on Implementation of the U.S. Space Exploration Policy, under which the four mission directorates and an Office of Education were established; space science and earth science are merged in a new Science Mission Directorate.

       The NASA Educator Astronaut Project (EAP) is established.

2005   Michael Griffin is named administrator of NASA.

       Angela Diaz is named NASA's assistant administrator for education.

2006   A new agencywide strategic plan is released, recasting the headquarters Office of Education as part of the Strategic Communications Office. The plan defines a set of goals for education programs throughout NASA.

       The management of Office of Education projects moves from headquarters to individual NASA centers.

       John Hairston is named NASA's acting assistant administrator for education (June).

       Joyce Winterton is named NASA's assistant administrator for education (October).

2007   A request for proposals (RFP) for the management of AESP is released.

2008   The Interdisciplinary National Science Project Incorporating Research and Education Experience (INSPIRE) is scheduled to begin.

During the tenure of Administrator Sean O'Keefe, December 2001–February 2005, the headquarters Office of Education was elevated from part of the Human Resources and Education Office to enterprise status. This move made the headquarters Office of Education comparable, organizationally, to the Space Science, Earth Science, Biological and Physical Research, Aerospace Technology, and Space Flight Enterprises (National Aeronautics and Space Administration, 2003a).

In 2002, Administrator O'Keefe named Dr. Adena Williams Loston to the position of associate administrator for education. Authority for overseeing and managing national or multiregional education programs, and for a common strategy for education projects in the science and technology enterprises and NASA centers became centralized in the Education Enterprise managed by Dr. Loston. During the period that the office had enterprise status (2002–2004), all elements of NASA were expected to work together as "one NASA" to achieve the agency's ten goals (National Aeronautics and Space Administration, 2003b, p. 8). The Education Enterprise and education programs in the science and technology enterprises were directed to help NASA in its mission to inspire the next generation of explorers, by inspiring and motivating students to pursue careers in science, technology, engineering, and mathematics and by engaging the public in shaping and sharing the experience of exploration and discovery. There were seven specific objectives under goals 6 and 7 (National Aeronautics and Space Administration, 2003b, pp. A13–14):

1. Improve student proficiency in STEM subjects by creating a culture of achievement, using educational programs, products, and services based on NASA's unique missions, discoveries, and innovations.
2. Motivate K-12+ students from diverse communities to pursue science and math courses and, ultimately, college degrees in STEM disciplines.
3. Enhance STEM instruction with the unique teaching tools and experiences that only NASA can provide, and that are compelling to educators and students.
4. Improve the capacity of higher education to provide for NASA, and the nation's, future science and technology workforce requirements.
5. Improve the capacity of science centers, museums, and other institutions, through the development of partnerships, with the goal of translating and delivering engaging NASA content.
6. Improve science literacy by engaging the public in NASA missions and discoveries, and in the resulting benefits, through such avenues as public programming, community outreach, mass media, and the Internet.

7. Increase public awareness and understanding of how research and innovations in aerospace technology affect and improve the quality of life.

From November 2002 to June 2003, during the O'Keefe administration, 104 of the projects in the Education Enterprise, of which 48 were elementary and secondary level projects, were subjected to an internal NASA review. The review made an assessment of the degree to which each project in the Education Enterprise was aligned with NASA's education objectives. That review, as well as subsequent reviews, helped reduce the gaps in NASA's program pipeline, winnow out the lower-ranked programs, and encourage programs ranked simply as "good," to strive for "excellence." The Science, Engineering, Mathematics and Aerospace Academy (SEMAA), NASA Explorer Schools (NES), Educator Astronaut Project (EAP), and Aerospace Education Services Project (AESP) were among the projects that received excellent and good ratings in those reviews.

Education Projects in the Science and Technology Enterprises

Most of the education projects in the science and technology enterprises were located in the Office of Space Science (OSS) and the Office of Earth Science (OES). These programs evolved somewhat independently of the programs in the Education Enterprise, but they represented a substantial portion of NASA's overall activity in K-12 education. For example, in fiscal 2003, the last year for which OSS published data, OSS reported sponsorship of more than 5,000 discrete events and the development of more than 50 new space science educational materials or resources (National Aeronautics and Space Administration, 2004a, p. 1).

The OSS strategic plan (National Aeronautics and Space Administration, 1995) and implementation plan (National Aeronautics and Space Administration, 1996) that guided the program were created in 1994–1996 through a series of planning activities that relied heavily on external experts in science education working under the guidance of the NASA Space Science Advisory Committee. The OSS funded four education projects: Initiative to Develop Education through Astronomy and Space Science (IDEAS), Mission Education and Public Outreach (EPO), education and public outreach supplements, and forums and broker/facilitators. Each program was contracted and funded differently, as described below.

The IDEAS grant project was an independent education and public outreach grant program not directly attached to a science research program. It provided start-up funding (ranging from $20,000 to $50,000) to explore innovative, creative ways to integrate astronomy and space science in U.S. education and public outreach venues, through partnerships between astronomers and space scientists and formal and informal education professionals.

The OSS Mission education and public outreach efforts were the product of a 1994 mandate that all NASA space science missions and research programs commit 1–2 percent of their resources to education and public outreach. Each mission was required to have an EPO program that emphasized direct involvement of the mission in carrying out EPO projects and mandated that all such activities be done in partnership with professional educators. Each mission also required that projects be leveraged to reach the maximum possible audience. Mission proposals were required to have an EPO component that was reviewed on the basis of those criteria, and that influenced the final decision regarding selection of the mission for funding.

Individual scientists funded by OSS for research could also apply for education and outreach supplements to develop and implement additional education projects. Proposals were awarded on a competitive basis; these projects were funded for smaller amounts than those that were part of the main mission education and outreach project.

To encourage and coordinate these activities, a support network comprising four theme-oriented education forums and seven regional broker-facilitators was established. The forums coordinated the efforts of individual space science missions, and the broker/facilitators assisted space scientists in becoming involved in education through the creation of partnerships with educators.

In contrast with the OSS program, the OES education program was a historically more modest and traditional suite of activities and resource materials (about 50–75 activities per year during 2001–2005), developed by NASA or by individual grantees through an open solicitation. These open solicitations funded projects in K-12, undergraduate, graduate, and informal science education. Funding of K-12 projects led to the development of such programs as the Global Learning and Observation to Benefit the Environment (GLOBE) Project and Earth Systems Science Education Alliance (ESSEA). The GLOBE Project is a partnership between NASA, the National Science Foundation, and the Department of State and draws on the various resources of the three agencies to engage primary and secondary students in hands-on data collection and analysis of the environment and the earth system. ESSEA is national program aimed at improving the knowledge, skills, and resources of K-12 earth systems science educators through online courses.

Education Projects in the NASA Centers

During this time period (1992–2005), the NASA centers played a central role in the implementation of agency-level education projects and also led the development of a small number of center-specific education projects. The primary responsibility of the centers was to implement national programs in a specified geographical region. At the precollege level, the education director at each center was (and continues to be) responsible for a specific geographic region, in order to ensure education staff members at the centers were familiar with and responsive to state and local education issues. The education staff was instructed to work closely with local and state education officers to support systemic reform initiatives in formal education, assist with the generation and communication of knowledge through the higher education infrastructure, and establish linkages with informal education networks in support of the agency's national science, technology, engineering, and mathematics initiatives (National Aeronautics and Space Administration, 2003a, p. 32).

Summary

The recent history of NASA's K-12 science, technology, engineering, and mathematics education is characterized by the wide number and variety of programs, projects, and activities, each implemented by different managers in different parts of the agency (e.g., the headquarters Office of Education, the center education offices, the mission education offices, the Human Resources Offices at the centers and at headquarters, and the Equal Opportunity Offices at the centers and at headquarters), as well as by universities and laboratories affiliated with NASA missions.

Recognizing that a more coherent system was needed, NASA has made an ongoing effort to pull these disparate parts of the education program together. However, the strategy for creating a more coherent education program has shifted with changes in administration in the agency. For example, since 2000, the education programs have been organized to align to three different agencywide strategic plans. By 2004, the number of enterprise-level program managers had grown to eight, with the addition of the Safety and Mission Assurance Enterprise and the Exploration Systems Enterprise. During the same year, the report of the President's Commission on Implementation of the U.S. Space Exploration Policy (President's Commission on Moon, Mars, and Beyond, 2004) recommended that NASA transform itself into a more focused and effectively integrated organization to implement the national space vision.

That report led to a new plan for NASA's organization, which restructured the agency's strategic enterprises into four mission directorates, reduced the number of functions reporting directly to the NASA administrator, and retained an Office of Education with responsibility for overseeing all education activities in NASA. A detailed description of these changes and their impact is provided in the following section.

CURRENT APPROACH

In April 2005, NASA Administrator Dr. Michael Griffin began his tenure with implementation of a new organizational structure and strategic plan for the agency. The new structure was guided by a post-Columbia review panel that recommended the integration of NASA's numerous offices and enterprises so that a smaller and more cohesive number of groups reported to the administrator. In the new organizational structure (see Figure 2-1), the headquarters Office of Education became a part of the Strategic Communications Office, along with external relations, legislative affairs, and public affairs. The new structure included four mission directorates (formerly science and technology enterprises): Exploration Systems Directorate, Space Operations Directorate, Science Directorate, and Aeronautics Research Directorate. The various projects previously managed by the headquarters Office of Education, while still officially Office of Education projects, would be managed instead by one of the NASA centers.

Education Strategic Coordination Framework

In 2006, in an effort to align with the new agencywide organizational structure and strategic plan, the headquarters Office of Education developed the "education strategic coordination framework" (National Aeronautics and Space Administration, 2006a). The framework states that NASA "is taking a leading role to inspire interest in science, technology, engineering, and mathematics, as few other organizations can through its unique mission, workforce, facilities, research, and innovations" (p. 3). It is significant that in this document, NASA cites not only the Space Act as an imperative for its involvement in education, but also imperatives derived from the report *Rising Above the Gathering Storm* (National Research Council, 2007a) These imperatives closely echo the Space Act:

> (1) increase America's talent pool by vastly improving K-12 science and mathematics education; (2) sustain and strengthen the Nation's traditional commitment to long-term basic research; (3) make the United States the most attractive setting in which to study and perform research; and (4) ensure that the United States is the premiere place in the world to innovate. (p. 3)

NASA's current goals in education, as laid out in the framework, address issues in workforce development, formal education, and informal education (National Aeronautics and Space Administration, 2006a):

- Strengthen NASA and the Nation's future workforce—NASA will identify and develop the critical skills and capabilities needed to ensure achievement of the Vision for Space Exploration. To help meet the

National Aeronautics and Space Administration

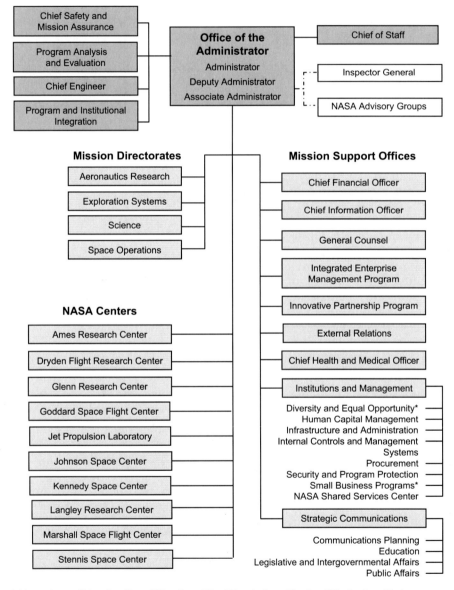

* In accordance with law, the offices of Diversity and Equal Opportunity and Small and Disadvantaged Business Utilization maintain reporting relationships to the Deputy Administrator and Administrator.

FIGURE 2-1 NASA organizational chart.
SOURCE: National Aeronautics and Space Administration, 2007.

demand, NASA will continue contributing to the development of the Nation's science, technology, engineering, and mathematics (STEM) workforce of the future through a diverse portfolio of education initiatives that target America's students at all levels, especially those in traditionally underserved and underrepresented communities.

- Attract and retain students in STEM disciplines—NASA will focus on engaging and retaining students in STEM education projects to encourage their pursuit of educational disciplines and careers critical to NASA's future engineering, scientific, and technical missions.

- Engage Americans in NASA's mission—NASA will build strategic partnerships and linkages between STEM formal and informal education providers. Through hands-on, interactive educational activities, NASA will engage students, educators, families, the general public, and all Agency stakeholders to increase Americans' science and technology literacy. (p. 4)

These goals, as well as the motivations that NASA cites for its overall involvement in education, are all consistent with national policy and the role this panel believes NASA should be playing in K-12 education. They are also consistent with the work of the Academic Competitiveness Council and its 2008 Planning Guidance for Math and Science Education Programs (U.S. Department of Education, 2007a).

Organization of Education Projects

All education programs in the headquarters Office of Education, the mission directorates, and the centers are expected to achieve at least one of the following three overarching outcomes:

Outcome 1: Contribute to the development of the STEM workforce in disciplines needed to achieve NASA's strategic goals, through a portfolio of investments.

Outcome 2: Attract and retain students in STEM disciplines through a progression of educational opportunities for students, teachers, and faculty.

Outcome 3: Build strategic partnerships and linkages between STEM formal and informal education providers that promote STEM literacy and awareness of NASA's mission.

To accomplish these outcomes, the framework describes a progressive series of stages, depicted as a pyramid, through which participants in NASA's education programs move. The four stages of the pyramid are: inspire, engage, educate, and employ; see Figure 2-2. The agency has adopted the language of "push and pull" to describe the ways that the wide array of NASA's education projects can work together to keep students moving forward. For example, projects at the high school level can "reach down" to connect with projects performed at the middle school level and "pull" students up to the next project. Similarly, projects at the elementary school level can work proactively to connect to projects for older students and "push" interested students to the next level of opportunity. The agency has begun to collect agencywide project participation data records, which may eventually allow it to track whether the education programs are operating as designed.

The education strategic coordination framework is also based on a philosophy that encourages diversity, as well as six overarching principles that contain elements essential to high-quality and successful education programs: relevance to the education community, content from NASA resources, diversity of participants, reliable evaluation, continuity from program to program, and partnerships with external partners.

Organizational and Management Structure

The organizational and management structure (Figure 2-3) derived from the new framework is designed to draw on NASA program content. The structure outlines specific roles for the assistant administrator for edu-

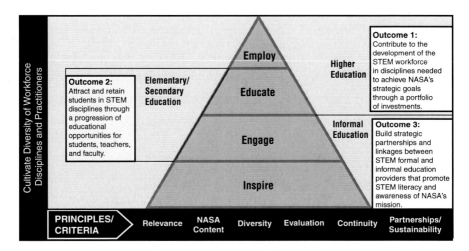

FIGURE 2-2 NASA education strategic coordination framework pyramid showing outcomes mapped to the education strategic framework.
SOURCE: National Aeronautics and Space Administration, 2006a, p. 7.

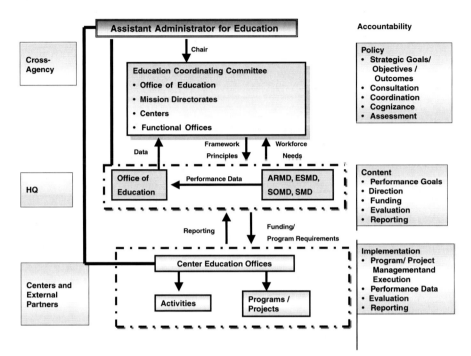

FIGURE 2-3 NASA education strategic coordination framework.
SOURCE: National Aeronautics and Space Administration, 2006a, p. 10.

cation, the ECC, the Office of Education, the mission directorates, and the center education offices.

The Assistant Administrator for Education

The assistant administrator for education has two major roles, as well as related responsibilities. First, the person leads the headquarters Office of Education and manages all of the related responsibilities. Second, as the chair of the ECC, the assistant administrator is responsible for the overall planning, coordination, and integration of NASA's education portfolio.

The Education Coordinating Committee

The education strategic coordination framework describes the ECC as a "collaborative structure to strategically manage the implementation of numerous programs, projects and activities in a distributed system"

(National Aeronautics and Space Administration, 2006a, p. 9). It comprises the assistant administrator for education, the deputy assistant administrator of education, the executive secretary to the committee, the mission directorate education leads, the education office directors of the centers, and representatives from various other NASA offices.

The group is tasked with providing an overarching agency structure in which issues can be discussed to guide the decision making of the assistant administrator for education. In addition, it is intended to integrate the diverse education projects across the agency into a coordinated portfolio; maintain awareness of all education projects and major milestones, evaluations, reviews, and investment plans; and establish evaluation criteria and review evaluation results. The Office of Education plans to convene the group on a monthly basis or as requested by the assistant administrator.

The Headquarters Office of Education

The headquarters Office of Education administers national education programs, performs institutional management tasks (e.g., ensures compliance with U.S. Office of Management and Budget and internal regulations, manages external inquiries), coordinates the implementation of the NASA education strategic framework approach, provides national partnership networks and infrastructure for dissemination, represents the agency externally, coordinates the evaluation and assessment of the agency education portfolio, and reports results to the ECC.

The Mission Directorates

The mission directorates embed education activities within their research and development programs and flight missions, ensure meaningful collaboration between the NASA science and engineering community and the education community, coordinate their programs with the headquarters Office of Education and the centers, ensure program evaluation using ECC criteria, and provide data to the central agency education database. The mission directorates may also develop education related partnerships specific to their disciplines and needs, including discipline-specific interactions with other federal agencies.

The Center Education Offices

The education offices in the ten NASA field centers (which include the Jet Propulsion Lab) are responsible for working with formal and informal education institutions and for involving colleges and universities to support the generation and communication of new scientific knowledge and advancements in engineering. The offices implement NASA education programs, projects, and activities for the mission directorates and the headquarters Office of Education, plan and implement center-funded education programs, provide expertise in defining K-12 state standards and requirements in their geographic area of responsibility, disseminate valuable field-based input for education program planning, and maintain records of all programs funded in their region. They report administratively to center management and functionally to the headquarters Office of Education.

The K-12 Education Portfolio

In the education strategic coordination framework, the K-12 education portfolio consists of the headquarters Office of Education projects, including the seven core projects that are the focus of this review, as well as mission directorate and center projects.

All K-12 projects are intended to focus primarily on attracting and retaining students in STEM disciplines (outcome 2 in the strategic framework). These projects cover the two middle stages of involvement in the pyramid: engage and educate (see Table 2-1). Engage activities are defined as activities that incorporate participant interaction with NASA science and engineering content. Educate activities are defined as activities that focus educational support through supplementary classroom and after-school activities that promote new knowledge and skill acquisition. K-12 projects are divided into four major categories: educator professional development of short duration, educator professional development of long duration (NASA defines long duration as more than two days), curricular support resources, and student involvement. Activities in each of the categories have been developed or funded by the headquarters Office of Education, the mission directorates, and the center education offices.

Elementary and Secondary Education Program

The headquarters Office of Education projects are organized into five programs: elementary and secondary education, higher education, informal education, e-Education, and the Minority University Research and Education Program (MUREP). Projects in the Elementary and Secondary Education Program and the Higher Education Program address multiple education issues and populations at specific K-12 grade levels and at higher education levels. The Informal Education Program and e-Education Program provide education services for various age groups and populations through specific venues (e.g., museums and the Internet). MUREP addresses educational issues of underserved and underrepresented students at both K-12 and higher education levels, through activities undertaken by minority universities.

TABLE 2-1 NASA Education Portfolio Activity Categories

Activity	Outcome	Description
Educator Professional Development— Short Duration	Engage	Provide short duration professional development and training opportunities to educators equipping them with the skills and knowledge to attract and retain students in STEM disciplines.
Educator Professional Development— Long Duration	Educate	Provide long-duration and/or sustained professional development training opportunities to educators that result in deeper content understanding and/or competence and confidence in teaching STEM disciplines.
Curricular Support Resources	Engage	Provide curricular support resources that use NASA themes and content to inform students about STEM career opportunities and communicate information about NASA mission activities.
Curricular Support Resources	Educate	Provide curricular support resources that use NASA themes and content to enhance student skills and proficiency in STEM disciplines.
Student Involvement K-12	Engage	Provide K-12 students with authentic first-hand opportunities to participate in NASA mission activities thus inspiring interest in STEM disciplines and careers.
Family Involvement	Engage	Provide opportunities for family involvement in K-12 student learning in STEM areas.

SOURCE: Internal Use Draft Elementary and Secondary Education Program Plan (June 21, 2006) and personal communication from Shelly Canright, outcome manager, Elementary and Secondary and e-Education Programs.

Overall, the majority of K-12 projects in the headquarters Office of Education are in the Elementary and Secondary Education Program, with a small number K-12 projects in the Informal Education Program, the e-Education Program, and MUREP. As noted in Chapter 1, this committee's study was focused primarily on the projects in the Elementary and Secondary Program.

In that program, as described in Chapter 1, the headquarters Office of Education has developed seven core projects: the Aerospace Education Services Project (AESP), the Science, Engineering, Mathematics and Aerospace Academy (SEMAA), the NASA Explorer Schools (NES), the Digital Learning Network (DLN, a component of NES), the Educator Astronaut Project (EAP), the Education Flight Projects (EFP), and the Interdisciplinary National Science Project Incorporating Research and Education Experience (INSPIRE). The projects include both formal and informal education activities designed for a wide variety of audiences (teachers, students, and families) and goals. They are congressionally funded and managed by centers with oversight from the headquarters Office of Education.

The budget for each project is determined each year as part of the President's budget. The headquarters Office of Education received $162 million in fiscal 2006, $29 million of which was directed to the Elementary and Secondary Program. Table 2-2 presents the most accurate available data on the headquarters Office of Education project budgets from fiscal 2003 to fiscal 2008. As the table illustrates, there has been a general decline in education funding across the Office of Education Programs, from $201 million in fiscal 2003 to $162 million in fiscal 2006, with three exceptions in 2004 (elementary and secondary, higher education, and informal education) and in 2006 for informal education. The budget request for 2007 funding for the headquarters Office of Education Program was comparable to 2006; the total 2008 budget request dropped substantially, to $121.9 million.

It is also noteworthy that congressionally directed appropriations (earmarks) account for a significant percentage of the Office of Education's total budget. In 2006, the total was $57.8 million (36%), an increase from only $3 million in 1996. More than one-half of the directed appropriations in fiscal 2006 were directed to the Informal Education Program: $32 million of the total $34 million budget, fully 93 percent. Without an increase in the headquarters Office of Education budget, congressionally directed appropriations limit the office's ability to allocate resources on the basis of an overall strategy for the Elementary and Secondary Program or the merits and needs of individual projects.

Mission Directorate Education Projects

The K-12 education projects in the mission directorates are not accounted for in the budget information discussed above. Most of these projects produce curriculum enhancement products, support professional development for teachers, or engage students in mission-related research activities. The investment in education by the mission directorates is meant to supplement what is done in the headquarters Office of Education, and there are some connections between the two sets of projects. For example, each year the mission directorates inform AESP officials of the materials that are available and of recent advances in their fields.

The level of investment in education activities varies across the four mission directorates. The Science Mission Directorate (SMD)—which was created from the merger of the former Office of Space Science (OSS) and the Office of Earth Science (OES)—manages the majority of mission director-

TABLE 2-2 Office of Education Funding by Program and Project for Fiscal 2003–2008 (in thousands)

Programs and Projects	Fiscal Budget				Budget Request	
	2003	2004	2005	2006	2007	2008
Elementary and Secondary						
NASA Educator Astronaut (NEA)	$60	$2,000	$1,776	$2,476	$2,900	$2,700
Aerospace Education Services Project (AESP)	8,728	6,272	2,191	3,791	6,300	5,300
Interdisciplinary National Program Incorporating Research and Education Experiences (INSPIRE)[a]	2,466	3,193	3,306	0	3,900	3,700
NASA Explorer Schools (NES)[b]	1,267	12,654	11,729	9,500	14,100	12,300
Science, Engineering, Mathematics and Aerospace Academy (SEMAA)[c]	6,642	4,935	4,360	4,845	4,200	4,000
NASA Student Involvement Program	639	1,235	34	0	0	0
Flight Projects	1,810	1,170	2,037	0	2,000	1,100
Small Programs	987	1,005	266	0	0	0
Education Program Support	5,898	16,606	7,015	225	0	0
Congressionally Directed Appropriations (site specific)	3,123	4,390	8,283	7,200	NA	NA
Corporate G&A[d]/Institutional Investments/Center M&O[e]	980	2,359	5,447	1,244	—	—
Subtotal	$32,600	$55,819	$46,444	$29,281	$33,400	$29,300
Higher Education						
Experimental Program to Stimulate Competitive Research[c]	$7,221	$9,350	$11,522	$12,340	$10,000	$10,000
Science and Technology Scholarship Project	NA	3,029	1,134	0	0	0
National Space Grant and College Fellowship Program[c]	23,778	24,920	26,201	29,806	28,800	29,000
Undergraduate Student Researchers Project	0	0	616	0	3,700	3,700
Graduate Student Researchers Project	7,388	6,168	4,040	4,875	8,700	8,700
NASA Faculty Fellowship Project	3,164	3,325	0	0	0	0
Congressionally Directed Appropriations (site specific)	28,184	27,089	14,283	17,856	NA	NA
Corporate G&A[d]/Institutional Investments/Center M&O[e]	2,926	4,942	3,839	4,295	—	—
Subtotal	$72,661	$78,823	$61,634	$69,172	$53,200	$52,500

e-Education						
Learning Technologies Project	$3,507	$2,025	$2,328	$1,482	$2,900	$1,900
NASA Education Technology Services	98	986	1,499	1,485	1,900	1,400
Classroom of the Future[c]	2,559	1,500	1,500	1,858	2,000	2,100
Small Programs	1,831	661	1,101	1,537	1,700	60
Congressionally Directed Appropriations (site specific)	2,999	3,456	496	1,252	NA	NA
Corporate G&A[d]/Institutional Investments/Center M&O[e]	556	576	1,442	524	—	—
Subtotal	$11,550	$9,204	$8,367	$8,138	$8,500	$5,500
Informal Education						
NASA Explorer Institutes	$400	$1,646	$1,944	$484	$2,400	$1,700
Congressionally Directed Appropriations (site specific)	6,048	10,673	10,912	31,567	NA	NA
Corporate G&A[d]/Institutional Investments/Center M&O[e]	587	883	319	1,941	—	—
Subtotal	$7,035	$13,202	$13,174	$33,992	$2,400	$1,700
MUREP						
Saturday Academies	$8,232	$970	$970	$0	$0	$0
Network Resources Training Sites	2,453	2,450	458	325	0	0
Model Institutions of Excellence	1,758	2,400	2,064	0	0	0
Partnerships Awards for Integration of Research	2,200	900	900	681	0	0
Institutional Research Awards	7,040	1,000	0	0	0	0
University Research Center	10,200	22,288	14,263	8,390	18,200	14,700
Faculty Awards for Research	4,225	3,537	2,779	995	1,800	4,400
Earth Science Collaboration	475	630	400	0	0	0
Curriculum Improvement Partnership Award	10,428	3,500	2,349	987	2,500	2,500
Space Science Collaboration	2,759	3,665	3,330	0	0	0
Math, Science Teacher and Curriculum Enhancement Program	93	1,995	533	0	0	0
Tribal Colleges and Universities	2,138	1,400	1,371	886	1,900	1,700
NASA Science and Technology Institute for Minority Institutions (was Research Academy)	991	727	1,194	558	1,200	1,100

continued

TABLE 2-2 Continued

Programs and Projects	Fiscal Budget				Budget Request	
	2003	2004	2005	2006	2007	2008
MUREP (continued)						
Undergraduate Scholars	8,100	7,495	3,532	1,969	0	0
Jenkins Post-doctoral Fellowship Project	1,069	2,800	2,531	1,974	2,600	2,600
NASA Administrator's Fellowship Project	4,225	2,500	2,375	1,974	2,500	2,500
Pre-college Achievement of Excellence	100	1,189	0	0	0	0
Texas Project Proyecto Access	879	1,000	0	0	0	0
Motivating Undergraduates in Science and Technology	NA	NA	NA	0	0	1,900
Small Programs	6,810	7,019	2,819	1,465	200	1,500
Congressionally Directed Appropriations (site specific)	0	0	0	0	NA	NA
Corporate G&A[d]/Institutional Investments/Center M&O[e]	3,253	5,893	7,424	1,569	—	
Subtotal	$77,428	$73,358	$49,293	$21,773	$34,440	$32,900
Total	$201,275	$230,405	$178,913	$162,356	$161,800	$121,900

NOTES: Amounts here do not reflect revised strategy for addressing full-cost recovery (i.e., full-cost simplification) which was implemented beginning in fiscal 2007. See also note to Table 3-1.

[a]Through fiscal 2005 this project was the Summer High School Apprenticeship Research Project (SHARP).
[b]Through fiscal 2006, this program was part of MUREP; the change was done to more appropriately align the project with the function program area addressed, elementary and secondary education.
[c]Includes congressionally directed appropriations.
[d]General and administrative costs.
[e]Management and operational costs.

SOURCES: Combined from multiple sources including personal communication, Malcom Phelps, director, Research and Evaluation, NASA Office of Education; National Aeronautics and Space Administration President's FY 2006 Budget Request; and National Aeronautics and Space Administration President's FY 2007 Budget Request. Available: http://www.nasa.gov/pdf/142458main_FY07_budget_full.pdf and FY 06: http://www.nasa.gov/pdf/107486main_FY06_high.pdf [accessed November 2007].

ate K-12 projects. The SMD has continued the former OSS public outreach tradition of mandating that all funded missions include a suite of related education activities done in partnership with professional educators. The education component of all mission and research proposals continues to be an integral part of the proposal review and selection process. SMD has also continued the OSS tradition of offering the opportunity for scientists who have been awarded individual science research grants to propose supplemental education funding, and the OES tradition of offering open solicitations for SMD-related science education projects.

The other mission directorates have much smaller K-12 education efforts. The Aeronautics Research Mission Directorate manages the set of educational programs previously offered by the former Office of Aeronautics. Their website lists a set of 12 educational publications or web-based resources for K-12 students and teachers. The websites of the Exploration Systems Mission Directorate and the Space Operations Mission Directorate do not show any specific education activities, largely because the Exploration Systems Mission Directorate is relatively new and has yet to develop an education program, and the Space Operations Directorate has historically not been expected to contribute to NASA's role in education because it has been perceived as an operations organization rather than a mission or research organization. It is important to keep these components in the picture because they offer another view of NASA's role in STEM education. For example, the Space Operations Directorate is an organization with much expertise in applied technology that could support education projects focused on engineering and technology.

An approximation of the total amount of education funding by the mission directorates was derived from work commissioned by the Office of Education from the Institutes for Global Environment Strategies. The executive summary for this report cautions that "the purpose of budget information reported through this data call was to develop an approximation of the NASA's funding within activity types, and should not be interpreted as a precise budget costs report" (Schwerin, 2006, p. 3). The report estimates that the mission directorate education projects received $83 million in fiscal 2006, approximately $35 million of which supported K-12 education activities. SMD has the largest education project budget among the mission directorates: nearly three-fourths of the total K-12 mission project funding (about $25 million).[2] This is nearly equal to the funding for the headquarters Office of Education's Elementary and Secondary Program ($29 million). As noted above, all SMD science missions must reserve a percentage of funds for education projects in its budget. As of the time this

---

[2]M. Wei (Education and Public Outreach Lead for the Science Mission Directorate) personal communication, May 7, 2007.

report was written, it was 0.25–0.50 percent, decreased from the 1–2 percent that was previously required under OSS. Funds are awarded through a competitive process either as an aspect of a proposal for a mission or as a proposal for an independent education activity.[3]

Center Education Projects

The NASA centers develop and implement a small number of projects, which are funded with the centers' discretionary funds, through outside sponsors, or from the headquarters Offices of Education and the mission directorates. Only a small percentage of these programs are targeted at K-12 students. For example, NASA supports the participation of high school teams in For Interest and Recognition of Science and Technology (FIRST) Robotics competitions, and the centers provide the needed funding and mentorship for local teams of high school students to participate.

As part of the recent change in management structure, responsibility for implementation of existing projects was competed across centers. Each center created a proposal that was reviewed by division heads, senior leadership, and assistant administrators within the agency, as well as by external experts. Recommendations from these four groups were taken into consideration in awarding project implementation responsibilities for each program. As a result, each project is currently managed by the center that was judged to have the most appropriate expertise and resources available.

SUMMARY

Throughout its history, NASA's many and varied education programs and projects have been initiated and implemented by a variety of offices at the headquarters and center levels. During 2001–2005, Administrator O'Keefe centralized management, first as the Education Enterprise and later as the Office of Education, with programs and projects implemented by headquarters staff. Since 2005, the approach of Administrator Griffin has been to reduce the headquarters staff and place the managerial responsibilities for NASA's elementary and secondary projects at the NASA centers, with each center having the lead responsibility for a particular education project. This change in the management of the headquarters Office of Education projects reflects the agencywide restructuring effort that has moved direct project management from headquarters to the centers. However, the headquarters Office of Education still retains responsibility for ensuring coherence and coordination among all NASA education projects.

---

[3]M. Wei (Education and Public Outreach Lead for the Science Mission Directorate) and L. Cooper, personal communication, May 7, 2007.

Under the 2006 education strategic coordination framework, the headquarters Office of Education assumes a planning, coordination, and compliance role as a support office under the chief of strategic communications. The office is specifically tasked to "draw on content from across the Agency," and to provide "national partnership networks and infrastructure to disseminate NASA education content and activities developed by the Mission Directorates, Centers, and education partners" (NASA, 2006a, p. 8).

The mission directorates and center education offices currently play a major role in the current K-12 education portfolio. The mission directorates are responsible for including education components in their research and development programs and flight missions, implementing the content-specific activities for which they provide funding, collaborating between the NASA science and engineering community and the education community, and providing performance data to the headquarters Office of Education. The center education offices are responsible for implementing NASA education projects, as well as planning and implementing center-funded education programs.

The headquarters Office of Education is trying to operate effectively while coping with fluctuations in organization and funding. However, the ongoing nature and frequency of such fluctuations has made it difficult for the agency to properly assess project quality or to develop long-term strategy and plans for evaluation.

3

The Federal Context for Education

Currently, there is strong national concern about the country's ability to meet the challenge of preparing a scientifically and technically capable workforce and a scientifically literate citizenry. These concerns have led to a focus on the quality of science, technology, engineering, and mathematics (STEM) education and on what can be done at the national level to improve the educational experiences and opportunities in STEM for students in grades K-12. Although federal science agencies, such as NASA, have an important role to play, they are often constrained by the focus of their overall mission, which is broader than just K-12 education. Furthermore, it is the individual states that have primary responsibility for K-12 public education and therefore play the primary role in defining and assessing K-12 education.[1]

In this chapter we first provide an overview of the role of the federal government in public K-12 STEM education. We then examine the roles of the Department of Education and the National Science Foundation, the two biggest federal funders of K-12 STEM education. Next, we look at the role of other federal science agencies in public K-12 STEM education. Finally, we discuss NASA's specific educational assets and how they help to define the agency's unique role in K-12 STEM education.

---

[1]At the undergraduate and graduate levels, which are not the focus of this report, it is generally assumed that the federal science agencies have a different and possibly broader role.

THE ROLE OF THE FEDERAL GOVERNMENT

The U.S. educational system is a complex structure consisting of many interrelated systems. Under the Constitution, it is the individual state governments, not the federal government that are responsible for K-12 public education (since it is not specified as a federal responsibility). The role that individual states play in governing education varies, with some states giving greater responsibility to county or local governments or both. That state and local responsibility is reflected in the funding for K-12 public school education: in 2005 about 90 percent of the total $536 billion spent on K-12 education came from state and local governments; only about 10 percent came from the federal government (U.S. Department of Education, 2006).

The involvement of the federal government in K-12 STEM education is relatively recent, dating back only to the mid-20th century. The federal government currently sets the national agenda in K-12 STEM education through two processes. First, it passes legislation that affects federal funding, which can lead to changes in state and local education systems. For example, Title I of the Elementary and Secondary Education Act, its reauthorization under the No Child Left Behind Act, implemented by the Department of Education, have had significant effects on K-12 STEM education. Second, Congress provides funding for federal agencies involved in K-12 STEM education, which influences the types of K-12 STEM education programs that are developed and supported by federal agencies.

Even though the influence of the federal government on education has grown, its authority over K-12 public education remains limited. The federal government does not set a national curriculum or mandate state or local participation in federal programs. States can refuse to participate in any federal education program (forgoing its associated funds). Yet however small the amounts of funding might be, the opportunity to receive federal financial support can influence the direction science education takes.

Many federal agencies, including the Department of Education, the National Science Foundation, the Department of Health and Human Services, the Department of Energy, the Department of Commerce, the Department of Agriculture, and the Department of Transportation, as well as NASA, fund K-12 STEM education programs and research.[2] These agencies share their expertise in science and science education through their involvement in education programs for students and teachers at the K-12 level. They develop programs that provide opportunities for learners to understand the nature of science, and they provide scientific knowledge, theory, and practice to educational institutions, both formal and informal,

---

[2]According to the report of the Academic Competitiveness Council, other agencies such as the Department of Defense, have significant involvement in STEM education but do not support projects whose primary focus is formal K-12 education.

through in-service teacher training[3] and curricular support material. Federally funded research on K-12 STEM education helps advance the understanding of student learning to determine how to improve teacher training and classroom settings and how to create more effective projects to support teachers and students. This research can also be used to inform the development of K-12 STEM education programs.

According to the Report of the Academic Competitiveness Council (U.S. Department of Education, 2007a), there are currently 12 federal agencies that provide funding for STEM education programs, 8 of which provide funds specifically for K-12 programs. The report says that in 2006 federal agencies spent $3.1 billion on STEM education, $574 million (18%) of which supported K-12 STEM programs. About 62 percent of the total federal STEM budget in 2006 supported programs identified as general STEM programs (including K-12, undergraduate, graduate, and informal), 37 percent supported science- and engineering-focused programs, and only 1 percent supported specific mathematics-focused programs.[4] NASA accounts for only 4 percent of federally sponsored K-12 STEM education. As shown in Table 3-1, about 85 percent of the federal funds for K-12 STEM in 2006 were provided by the Department of Education and the National Science Foundation (about 42% each).

The role of federal agencies in supporting K-12 STEM education has been reviewed by two federal cross-agency panels since 1993 (the Federal Coordinating Council on Science, Engineering and Technology and the Academic Competitiveness Council). As described in Chapter 1, these reviews found that federal agencies have an important role in developing K-12 STEM programs and supporting research that addresses student learning, student engagement, and teacher quality. Both federal panels stressed the need for collaboration and evaluation. They recommended that federal agencies develop and sustain a culture of interaction, communication, and coordination across the agencies; that they strive to coordinate their efforts with state and local K-12 STEM education systems; and that they carry out evaluations to assess the impact of their programs and make changes to programs based on the evaluation findings (Federal Coordinating Council on Science, Engineering and Technology, 1993; U.S. Department of Education, 2007a). Both panels concluded that the federal agencies have an important role in K-12 STEM education, but they did not indicate what specific role each of the federal agencies should play. The differences in

---

[3]Preservice teacher education activities are categorized by the Department of Education as higher education activities.

[4]Federal funding of mathematics education may exceed 1 percent because general STEM programs may include mathematics (U.S. Department of Education, 2007a, p. 22).

TABLE 3-1 K-12 STEM Education Program Funding by Agency

Agency	2005 Funding	2006 Funding	2007 Request
Department of Agriculture	1,722,000	1,846,350	1,732,000
Department of Commerce	7,917,000	11,589,000	1,000,000
Department of Education	340,617,984	238,592,000	619,335,000
Department of Energy	3,944,000	4,340,000	5,645,000
Department of Health and Human Services	52,258,378	52,022,464	48,930,808
Department of Transportation	0	1,352,500	1,519,500
National Aeronautics and Space Administration	35,500,000	23,000,000	56,200,000
National Science Foundation	252,110,000	241,600,000	223,000,000
Total, K-12 Programs	$694,069,362	$574,342,314	$957,362,308

NOTE: Differences between NASA budget amounts in Tables 2-2 and 3-1 are due to the manner in which the American Competitiveness Council defines K-12 STEM education programs, which influenced which NASA headquarters Office of Education K-12 projects were included in its budget summary.
SOURCE: U.S. Department of Education, 2007a, p. 22.

agencies' missions, staff expertise, and budgets suggest that they have different capabilities and should play different roles in K-12 STEM education.

THE DEPARTMENT OF EDUCATION AND THE NATIONAL SCIENCE FOUNDATION

The Department of Education (DoED) and the National Science Foundation (NSF) play the largest role among the federal agencies involved in K-12 STEM education. The DoEd and NSF Directorate for Education and Human Resources (EHR) are the primary federal funders of K-12 STEM education programs and research. Their missions are specifically focused on education, although neither agency actually does science or engineering work in house. The DoEd is an education agency that supports K-12 STEM programs as part of its overall education mission. NSF is a science agency, and EHR is primarily focused on STEM education. Thus, these two agencies play different but significant roles in the K-12 STEM education system.

We believe it is important for other federal science agencies to be aware of the roles of these two agencies in order to minimize duplication of effort and to maximize awareness of the larger context in which their own programs are situated. Furthermore, the education programs, research, and services supported by the DoED and the NSF-EHR can be considered resources for the development of programs within the other federal science agencies.

The Department of Education

The Department of Education was established by Congress as a separate, cabinet-level department in 1980, taking over the functions and programs of its forerunner agency, the Office of Education (which was part of the Department of Health, Education, and Welfare). Its mission is to "promote student achievement and preparation for global competitiveness by fostering educational excellence and ensuring equal access" for all Americans. The department supplements and complements the efforts of states, local school systems, and other entities to improve the quality of education throughout the nation and increase the accountability of federal education programs (U.S. Department of Education, 2007b). Currently, the DoEd's primary influence over K-12 STEM education is through the No Child Left Behind Act (NCLB) and the Education Sciences Reform Act of 2002.

The 2001 reauthorization of the Elementary and Secondary Education Act (ESEA) under NCLB has had a broad impact on the K-12 education system. In general, NCLB has placed greater emphasis on accountability through assessments of basic skills, particularly in reading, mathematics, and science. The legislation also emphasizes the need for "highly qualified" teachers in core academic subjects. The emphasis on accountability and highly qualified teachers has influenced what, how, and when STEM topics are covered in elementary and secondary schools.

NCLB has also led to the funding of a small number of K-12 STEM-specific programs. However, overall, the department's investment in K-12 STEM-specific education programs ($238 million) represents less than 1 percent of its total 2006 investment in K-12 education ($36.5 billion). Most of the department's K-12 STEM education budget (about 75%) was allocated to the Math and Science Partnership (MSP) Program, a formula grant program (U.S. Department of Education, 2007a). The MSP Program, authorized under NCLB Title II, supports partnerships between the mathematics, science, or engineering faculty of institutions of higher education and high school districts to improve science and mathematics teachers' content knowledge and pedagogical skills. The activities of the MSP Program were formerly funded at a higher level under the Eisenhower Program.

DoEd continues its support and involvement in education research through the Institute for Education Sciences (IES), established under the Education Science Reform Act of 2002. IES comprises four centers: the National Center for Education Research (NCER), the National Center for Special Education Research (NCSER), the National Center for Education Statistics (NCES), and the National Center for Education Evaluation and Regional Assistance (NCEE). The two research centers (NCER and NCSER) provide research grants to develop rigorous evidence on which to ground general and special education practice and policy. NCER requests for research applications cover a wide array of educational issues, including such K-12 STEM-related issues as cognition and student learning, curricular and instructional approaches, and teacher professional development. Grant applications are solicited yearly and are awarded on a competitive basis.

NCES collects and provides information on the condition of education at all levels. It also produces STEM-specific reports at a national level, such as the National Assessment of Educational Progress (NAEP) science and math reports. NCEE conducts evaluations of the effects of federal programs and supports 10 regional education labs. The regional labs address student achievement by providing access to high-quality, scientifically valid education research through applied research and development projects, studies, and other related technical assistance activities. Only a small percentage of the NCEE evaluation and regional lab activities are specific to STEM education.

The National Science Foundation

The National Science Foundation (NSF), a federal science agency created by Congress in 1950, funds research in almost all areas of science and engineering. It has had a specific focus on STEM education from the outset, first in graduate and undergraduate education, and then, following the launching of Sputnik in 1957, at the K-12 level. Within NSF, K-12 STEM education is primarily the responsibility of the Directorate for Education and Human Resources (EHR). EHR provides limited-term grants for education research, innovative curriculum development and pedagogy, teacher professional development, education programs and activities, and other educational initiatives. EHR's budget was about $797 million in 2006, of which about $242 million (30%) supported K-12 education research. Other directorates in the NSF also support a small number of K-12 STEM education initiatives.[5]

Unlike other federal science agencies, such as NASA, NSF (including EHR) does not hire its own researchers or scientists or directly operate its own laboratories. Rather, its goal is to identify and support leading researchers and projects to carry out work in areas it deems important. Most grants are awarded to small groups of investigators, with a small frac-

---

[5]The NSF science directorates (including geosciences, biological sciences, engineering, and mathematics and physical sciences) support K-12 STEM education through research grants that require recipients to allocate a proportion of the budget to support the "broader impact" related to the research they sponsor. These broader impact funds are sometimes used to support education programs run by the grantees. For example, the Directorate for the Geosciences has allocated a portion of its funding to support educational activities that complement efforts by EHR, establish effective models of science education programs that can be scaled up or replicated, and leverage the directorate's research investments.

tion awarded to research centers or to provide instruments and facilities. For example, EHR has funded large-scale curriculum development projects to provide schools and districts with access to research-based and user-tested science curriculum resources, as well as professional development.

In the 1990s, EHR, concerned that years of investment in curriculum development and teacher training had not yielded the hoped-for level of improvement in science and mathematics education, changed its course to support "systemic reform" efforts that targeted large regions or states. Through this reform, the agency attempted to create coordinated efforts to improve science and mathematics teaching throughout targeted regional systems and structures. Over time, the original statewide targets changed to targets of urban or rural regional projects and then to "local systemic reform" projects involving one large or several smaller school districts. However, even with its relatively large budget, EHR does not have the capacity to initiate programs in all of the nation's schools.

In 2002, EHR began supporting teams composed of institutions of higher education, local K-12 school systems, and their partners through the Mathematics and Science Partnership (MSP) Program. The MSP program supported through NSF, funded at $63 million in 2006, is smaller than that supported by the Department of Education. Most recently, EHR has increased attention to research on learning and teaching and has reorganized its grant programs related to K-12 into a single Division for Research on Learning in Formal and Informal Settings.

THE ROLES OF OTHER SCIENCE AGENCIES

Given the major contributions of the DoEd and the NSF, what role is played by other federal agencies in work related to K-12 STEM education? What additional contributions might they make, and what need is there for cross-agency agreements and coordination to maximize impact? The answers to these questions differ slightly for each agency. The role that each plays is grounded in the legislation that defines its individual mission and in the fact that each is an employer of scientists, mathematicians, and engineers and a supporter of the research based in universities and research organizations.

The questions then become: What role should these scientists and engineers, and the scientific and technological contributions they make, play in aiding STEM educators at the K-12 level? How can these resources be used most effectively? Again, these questions must be addressed by each individual agency in its own way. However, certain aspects of how the different agencies strive to make valid contributions to K-12 STEM education are common across agencies. This section briefly discusses three of those aspects: the reasons for agency involvement, their resources, and the limitations of their involvement.

Reasons for Agency Involvement

Many federal science agencies are involved in training the next generation of engineers, technologists, and scientists at the graduate level, where supporting education and supporting research are closely connected. However, research suggests that the seed for student interest in science, mathematics, technology, and engineering careers must be planted during childhood and cultivated through effective educational opportunities at every stage along the path to a career in STEM (Tai et al., 2006). As a result, many federal agencies other than DoED and NSF-EHR see their involvement in K-12 education as part of an effort to keep students in the STEM pipeline and to produce a strong workforce that might some day contribute to their own fields of work. In addition to NASA, those agencies include the Department of Health and Human Services, the Department of Agriculture, the Department of Energy, the Department of Transportation, and the Department of Commerce, particularly the National Oceanic and Atmospheric Administration.

A second reason for many federal science agencies' involvement in K-12 STEM education is their commitment to repaying the American public for their support of agency-related science and engineering work. For example, much of the "value added" by NASA, especially in regard to its science missions, are advancements in human knowledge. Those advancements need to be made accessible to the public as well as to other scientists. In other words, federal agencies see a responsibility to support or develop programs that seek to increase the nation's scientific literacy. The goal is not to give each citizen the ability to make judgments about purely scientific issues, but rather to give all citizens enough basic knowledge to allow them to participate in public discourse on issues related to science. Although those issues usually also involve questions of economics, ethics, moral philosophy, or any of a number of other subjects, knowledge of the basic science is critical. For example, if a person does not have some knowledge of the complex set of scientific factors that influence the earth's climate, whatever his or her personal values, it would be hard to thoughtfully participate in discussions on issues related to alternative fuels and global warming. In this sense, one can think of scientific literacy as the necessary "ticket" that provides access to the civic arena.

Resources That Enable Agency Involvement

From the perspective of sharing knowledge about science, federal science agencies have two key resources that they can leverage to support K-12 STEM education. The first resource is the agencies' knowledge: that is, agencies "have the science." They produce cutting-edge research and engineering, thus contributing compelling data and ideas that are valuable resources to K-12 educators. As public agencies, they have a responsibility to promulgate this information and to make sure that the public, and educators in particular, have access to what they have learned. In some cases, the data itself can be made available in ways that allow students to interact with it in meaningful scientific investigations, thereby providing students with a window on the world of science that goes far beyond that of classroom investigations and school laboratories.

The second resource is the agencies' access to working scientists and engineers, both their own employees and the large numbers of researchers whom they support. Agency-supported scientists and engineers can play an important role in ensuring that education curricula present science, the scientific process, engineering, and the process of design and development in ways that engage students; correctly model the ways in which science and engineering are actually done; and provide educators and their students with accurate and up-to-date information. Agency education programs can capitalize on this unique asset and involve their scientists in modeling the nature of science and engineering and in improving teacher understanding of the science content they teach. Scientists and engineers can also be used as role models for students, sharing their enthusiasm for their work and its challenges and allowing students a real-world glimpse of the possibilities that such careers might offer.

Limitations of Agency Involvement

Federal science agencies have expertise in science and engineering, but they have limited expertise in education and in research on teaching and learning. In all their education efforts, agencies need to be informed by the best available knowledge about what is effective in education and how their programs contribute to a larger national education effort. The best way to achieve this marriage of science and education is for agency scientists and engineers to partner with people who are experienced in education (such as state and local leaders in STEM education), knowledgeable about research on learning, and who understand the educational landscape much in the same way that scientists and engineers understand their own.

Organizations of professional educators, such as the National Science Teachers Association and the Association of Science Technology Centers, are key resources for knowledge of the specific needs of classroom teachers and planetariums, museums, and science centers. Experienced curriculum development and professional development organizations know how to produce and disseminate educational materials that are both effective and compatible with national and state science education standards. State and local STEM education leaders can provide knowledge about the regional education systems, standards, and needs. Agencies need to be attentive to opportunities to develop contractual or partnership relationships that build on the expertise of people and groups knowledgeable about K-12 STEM education.

The role of federal science agencies in K-12 STEM education is also limited in terms of the breadth and depth of the initiatives that they can undertake. Federal science agencies are not in a position to independently develop and support programs that affect teaching practices, student learning, or systemic reform at a level that would result in national change. Even efforts by the largest federal agencies are dwarfed by the number and variety of school systems in the United States. Agency projects are therefore faced with striking a difficult balance between trying to make a broad impact while still providing meaningful engagement on a smaller scale. This balance can be mediated through modern technology, such as the Internet, which can be used as a distribution tool, and through strategic partnering with other federal science agencies and education organizations.

The need for and impact of such coordination is supported by recent and past reviews of federal STEM programs that found a considerable overlap across programs, the report of the Federal Coordinating Council for Science, Engineering and Technology (1993) and the report of the Academic Competitiveness Council (U.S. Department of Education, 2007a). Given "the extent of the STEM challenge and the unique contributions of each agency" (U.S. Department of Education, 2007a, p. 28), agencies that focus on similar areas of STEM and have developed parallel programs could benefit from the sharing of knowledge and coordination of efforts.

The organizational overhead of attempting to coordinate programs across agencies, or even within the entire distributed system of a single agency, can be high. Interagency work makes the most sense where common science interests drive it, particularly where there is science collaboration as well. In such situations, the pooling of resources can expand the reach and improve the quality of an agency's K-12 STEM education programs. For example, the Global Learning and Observation to Benefit the Environment (GLOBE) project, which is a partnership between NASA, NSF, and the Department of State, draws on the relevant resources of the three sponsoring agencies and a number of collaborating agencies and organizations to engage primary and secondary students in hands-on data collection and analysis of the environment and the earth system. The program's vision is to create an international community of students, teachers, scientists, and citizens working together to better understand the earth's environment. To achieve this vision, the program aims to engage students in "real" science, to improve students' understanding of science, to help students and teachers meet local educational goals, and to increase student awareness of the environment from a scientific viewpoint. The collaboration of the sponsoring agencies has made the international scope of this project a reality (Penuel and Means, 1999).

The role of every federal agency is also limited by the fact that programs must be matched to the primary mission(s) of the agency. If an agency embarks on a program that has little or nothing to do with its mission, it will be acting in an area where the agency staff has no inherent expertise. The resulting project is unlikely to be sustained. Conversely, shifts in the primary mission of an agency as a whole can affect its education programs, especially those with long-term objectives. Radical shifts, due for example to changes in administration or changes in agency priorities, can result in lack of stability in education programs and erratic funding that can seriously diminish the program's effectiveness. A funding pattern that fluctuates with federal and agency priorities can hamper the development and maintenance of effective education work in NASA and in other federal science agencies.

The roles and limitations described above apply to all of the federal agencies that support K-12 STEM education. The manner in which these agencies address these roles varies depending on the agency's mission, expertise, and funding.

NASA'S ROLE IN K-12 STEM EDUCATION

NASA's original charter in 1958 gives the agency the responsibility of managing U.S. civilian aeronautical and space activities for "peaceful purposes for the benefit of all mankind." Those purposes specifically include

> the expansion of human knowledge of phenomena in the atmosphere and space, the preservation of the role of the United States as a leader in aeronautical and space science and technology . . . [and] the most effective utilization of the scientific and engineering resources of the United States, with close cooperation among all interested agencies of the United States in order to avoid unnecessary duplication of effort, facilities, and equipment.

With the exception of having "knowledge of the earth" added to its responsibilities, these purposes have remained unchanged through all subsequent amendments to the original charter.

Taken together, these purposes can be used to define three major roles for NASA in science education. First, "expansion of human knowledge" requires the widest practicable dissemination of information about NASA's activities and the results and discoveries from its missions. Second, "preservation of . . . the United States as a leader in aeronautical and space science and technology" requires constant attention to inspiring and training the next generation of scientists and technologists. Third, "effective utilization of the scientific and engineering resources of the United States, with close cooperation among all interested agencies . . . to avoid unnecessary duplication of effort" implies a role for NASA as a partner in providing knowledge and expertise about the earth, aeronautics, and space to augment the efforts of the agencies that have primary responsibility for the nation's science education programs. Indeed, NASA's role in education was underscored in the 2001 review of the NASA education portfolio. The report concluded that NASA has "fiduciary and moral responsibilities to transfer and translate the knowledge gained from sophisticated science and engineering ventures into compelling educational experiences for students, teachers, and faculty throughout the nation" (Westat, 2001, p. 3).

Although NASA clearly has an important role to play in STEM education, the agency does not have the primary responsibility for overseeing, establishing, improving, or setting the agendas for STEM education in the United States. As described above, to the extent that there is a federal role in K-12 STEM education, the primary role is filled by the Department of Education and by the Directorate for Education and Human Resources of the National Science Foundation. NASA receives only a small portion (4%) of the federal funding of K-12 STEM education, and it is only one of several scientific and research federal agencies that have missions and resources that are charged with a role in science education.

Yet NASA is uniquely positioned to contribute to the nation's STEM education programs with its awe-inspiring facilities and missions; the data, images, and findings from five decades of space missions; and the scientists and engineers employed by the agency. Furthermore, NASA is the most publicly recognizable federal mission agency (Hopkins, 2007b) and has great public access through print, television, and web media. In K-12 STEM education, NASA can provide a unique set of opportunities linked to its science and engineering missions. The agency has the capacity to develop programs that address both general and specific topics in K-12 STEM education. NASA supports a collection of pioneering science and engineering missions and a roster of scientists and engineers, all of which can play a critical role in K-12 STEM education. NASA can share the manner in which its scientists and engineers pursue their innovative work with teachers and students, thus bringing the workings of science and engineering, as well as the products, into the classroom.

NASA is affiliated with a small number of precollege STEM education projects that support and encourage promising students to study STEM-related subjects throughout high school and college. Such projects have the potential to influence the scientific and technological literacy of teachers and students and to contribute to the development of a scientifically and technologically literate workforce, for NASA and throughout the U.S. economy.

NASA may be particularly well positioned to increase interest in technology and engineering. Although the term "STEM education" is often used for the K-12 level in U.S. education, there is historically very little focus in K-12 curricula and in the education programs of federal agencies on the technology and engineering components of the acronym. NASA's expertise in engineering could contribute to helping to fill the gap. With the challenges and lessons learned from designing and building spacecraft and advanced flight systems, NASA could bring the topic of technological challenges and the processes of engineering design to K-12 STEM education.

NASA is more widely known to the U.S. public than any other federal science agency and associated in the public mind with the challenges and excitement of space exploration (Hopkins, 2007b). The high level of public interest generated by its missions means that NASA has the capability to inspire students in a way that other education-related agencies or institutions cannot. There is no doubt that the thrill of space exploration can act as a magnet to attract public interest in science. Downloading the latest pictures from the surface of Mars or from the Hubble Space Telescope can be a catalyst for the eventual formulation of deeper questions: Was there ever life on Mars? How do you design a vehicle that can cross the terrain of Mars? What drives the expansion of the universe? The exploration of these questions may lead to greater interest in and future engagement in science and engineering topics. The inspirational role NASA plays with the public has the potential to draw students to the pursuit of academic study and eventual careers in STEM areas and thus makes NASA a valuable player in STEM education.

The agency's access to the public through print, television, and electronic media also affords it a distinctive opportunity to engage and interest students in aerospace science and engineering. For example, television coverage of a Mars Rover and the pictures it sends back can draw millions of viewers. When this coverage is supplemented by a well-designed web presence that provides teachers and students with access to more in-depth exploration of the data and what the scientists are learning from their work, it can become a rich and widely available educational resource. NASA uses this approach to share the excitement and the discoveries of its missions (National Research Council, 2007c).

4

Analysis of NASA's
K-12 Education Portfolio

In this chapter we present our analysis of NASA's portfolio in K-12 science, technology, engineering, and mathematics (STEM) education with particular attention to program design and effectiveness. The committee reviewed the seven core projects in the headquarters Office of Education Elementary and Secondary Program in depth: the Aerospace Education Services Project; NASA Explorer Schools; Digital Learning Network; Science, Engineering, Math and Aerospace Academy; the Education Flight Projects; Educator Astronaut Project; and the Interdisciplinary National Science Project Incorporating Research and Education Experience (INSPIRE).

The committee also reviewed some of the projects and activities in the Science Mission Directorate (SMD). Our review of the Science Mission Directorate projects was less detailed, as an in-depth review of such a large portfolio was beyond the scope of our study. The committee did believe it was necessary to give some attention to the SMD projects; however, because they represent approximately one-half of the agency's funding in K-12 education. Including these projects in the review gave the committee a better overall perspective of the scope of the agency's work at the precollege level. This chapter does not include analysis of individual SMD projects; however, we do discuss the general approach to education projects used in SMD and mention individual projects as examples.

The committee used several strategies for reviewing the seven core projects. We received briefings from NASA staff on each project, and we reviewed administrative documents, annual reports, and recent external evaluations. Committee members also drew on their knowledge of research in K-12 education regarding best practices in developing students' interests in science, technology, engineering, and mathematics; curriculum and instruction; and professional development as a framework against which to compare NASA K-12 projects. This expert knowledge was critical for the committee analysis because of the limitations of existing project evaluations. These limitations are not unique to NASA but are reflected across many federal science agencies involved in STEM education: see the report of the Academic Competitiveness Council (U.S. Department of Education, 2007a); also see Chapter 5 for an in-depth discussion of evaluation.

From its analyses of individual projects, the committee identified three areas in which NASA can improve the quality of its K-12 education program: project design and improvement, use of expertise in education, and the connection to the science and engineering in the agency. Before presenting our analysis, we lay out the frameworks that guided that analysis.

FRAMEWORK FOR BEST PRACTICE

From its review of research and the members' expertise, the committee identified three major topics that connect to NASA's program goals and encompass most of the activities of the constituent projects: developing interest; curriculum and instruction; and professional development for teachers. For each of these topics, the committee identified major conclusions that can be drawn from the research evidence regarding principles for best practice. In the following section, we briefly review these principles, which are then used as a framework for the critique of the constituent projects.

Developing and Sustaining Interest

Inspiring, engaging, and sustaining the interest of teachers and students in STEM subjects is one of the main goals of NASA's current education program, and is one of the greatest contributions that NASA can make to K-12 STEM education. The excitement generated by space flight and exploration puts NASA in a unique position to draw teachers and students into science, technology, engineering, and mathematics and related fields. However, of equal importance to the need to attract the interest of teachers and students is the need to sustain that interest over time and to link it to meaningful science content.

Substantial research has been done on the development of students' and teachers' motivations and interests, with some attention to how to design learning experiences that are both engaging and that result in real learning. In this research, "interest" is defined as both a positive feeling for science and the predisposition to continue to engage in science (Hidi and Renninger, 2006). Interest, in this sense, includes the stored knowledge, stored values, and feelings that influence the engagement, questioning, and activity of individuals (or groups of individuals). Interest has positive consequences for learning. For example, when people—both young and old—have a real interest in science, they are more likely to pose questions out of curiosity, seek out challenges, and use effective learning strategies (Barron, 2006; Csikzentmihayli, Rathunde, and Whalen, 1993; Engle and Conant, 2002; Kuhn and Franklin, 2006; Lipstein and Renninger, 2006; Renninger, 2000; Renninger and Hidi, 2002).

Early on, interest may be primarily triggered or maintained by external experience. As interest develops and deepens, however, a person is more likely to initiate engagement and to generate and seek answers to questions about content (Renninger, 2000). NASA's program in K-12 STEM education has the potential to trigger initial interest in students and teachers, as well as to provide experiences to deepen engagement for those who already have some initial interest. Two challenges for NASA in designing activities to "inspire and engage" are to attend to what is needed to translate initial excitement into a meaningful learning experience and a sustained, long-term interest and to support teachers in providing appropriate follow-up activities for an initial activity.

Reaching and engaging students who are typically underrepresented in STEM fields is a challenge that many of NASA's programs, particularly those managed by headquarters Office of Education, are designed to address. Although research on the most effective ways to bring underrepresented populations into STEM fields is thin, the evidence does suggest guidelines for best practice (BEST, 2004; Hall, 2007). One set of best practices was developed by the Building Engineering and Science Talent Initiative (BEST, 2004) through an expert review of programs. The practices include

- Defined outcomes: Students and educational staff agree on goals and outcomes. Success is measured against the intended results. Outcome data provide both quantitative and qualitative information. Disaggregated outcomes provide a basis for research and continuous improvement.
- Persistence: Effective interventions take hold, produce results, adapt to changing circumstances and persevere in the face of setbacks. Conditions that ensure persistence include proactive leadership, sufficient resources, and support at the district and school levels.
- Personalization: Student-centered teaching and learning methods are core approaches. Mentoring, tutoring, and peer interaction are integral parts of the learning environment. Individual differences, uniqueness, and diversity are recognized and honored.
- Challenging content: Curriculum is clearly defined and understood. Content goes beyond minimum competencies; relates to real-world applications and career opportunities and reflects local, state, and

national standards. Students understand the link between content rigor and career opportunities. Appropriate academic remediation is readily available.

- Engaged adults: Adults provide support, stimulate interest, and create expectations that are fundamental to the intervention. Educators play multiple roles as teachers, coaches, mentors, tutors, and counselors. Teachers develop and maintain quality interactions with students and each other. Active family support is sought and established.

A flexible program structure and opportunities for students to work in groups and socialize are also important based on a literature review commissioned by the committee (Hall, 2007).

Curriculum and Instruction

Many of NASA's contributions in K-12 STEM education fall under the category of curriculum materials and instructional activities. NASA seeks to provide curricular support resources that "use NASA themes and content to enhance student skills and proficiency in STEM disciplines, inform students about STEM career opportunities, and communicate information about NASA's mission activities" (National Aeronautics and Space Administration, 2006c).

Science curricula, for the purposes of this discussion, are defined as having three components: curriculum standards, curriculum materials, and instructional activities. Curriculum standards are the learning goals established collectively by national standards, state science expectations (e.g., state standards, state core curriculums, state expected learning outcomes), and district science curriculum guidance (e.g., guidelines, blueprints, learning expectations). Curriculum materials include textbooks, materials or labs, videos and other audio-visual materials, and reading materials. Instructional activities comprise the lesson plans, students' laboratory and field experiences, and modeling activities. NASA's work in K-12 STEM education focuses on curriculum materials designed to support NASA-related instructional activities. A teacher's decision to incorporate those activities should be informed by the curriculum and standards that apply for the course in question.

Curriculum standards lay out the science content and processes essential for science literacy and preparation for STEM pursuits. They provide a blueprint for the development of essential knowledge and skills and cultivation of scientific habits of mind for all students. The key role of curriculum standards is to bring coherence, articulation, and focus to instruction. Over the last 10–15 years there has been a movement toward creating standards at the national and state level that provide a framework to guide educators at the local level (National Research Council, 2007b). NASA has recognized this movement and has taken steps in its work with schools to show how the materials the agency offers are aligned with national and state standards.

In general, curriculum materials should, at a minimum, meet four criteria to be useful in improving student learning and achievement:

1. They should be aligned to the specific instructional objectives of the state and district standards.
2. They should be pedagogically sound.
3. They should be engaging and relevant.
4. They should be accurate in their presentation of scientific information.

The *National Science Education Standards* suggest that "[e]ffective science curriculum materials are developed by teams of experienced teachers, scientists, and science curriculum specialists using a systematic research and development process that involves repeated cycles of design, trial teaching with children, evaluation, and revision" (National Research Council, 1995, p. 213).

Research also shows that successful implementation of curriculum or of particular instructional activities and strategies usually requires some form of professional development for teachers. Indeed, increasing the effective use of high-quality instructional materials is at the center of many educational reform efforts. The National Science Foundation's Local Systemic Change in Mathematic and Science Program stressed the importance of the use of quality instructional materials with linked professional development. The evaluation of this program found that extensive use of even first rate instructional materials was effective only when linked to professional development targeted at teachers' practice, investigation, problem-solving, and instruction (Banilower et al., 2006).

Michael Lach, director of Mathematics and Science for the Chicago Public Schools, in his remarks to Congress on May 15, 2007, emphasized that professional development should focus not only on content, but also on effective instruction of that content.

> [A] picture emerges about the sort of work that isn't very helpful. Curriculum development is one. We know from decades of instructional material development that writing curriculum is a complicated, difficult process. We know that robust curriculum is necessary but not sufficient for classroom improvement. In addition to strong materials, teachers need equipment, professional development workshops, coaching, and good assessments. . . . Collections of lesson plans, by themselves, are only a small piece of the puzzle. (Lach, 2007, p. 4)

Teacher Enhancement and Professional Development

Professional development is clearly important for supporting effective implementation of the many curriculum resource materials developed by NASA for K-12 STEM education. Indeed, many projects incorporate activities aimed at increasing teachers' familiarity with NASA's resources and providing them with guidance on implementation.

Research on the effectiveness of combining teacher professional development with accepted best practices in the field provide clear guidelines for the design of quality professional development. For example, the recent report, *Taking Science to School,* identified several features of well-structured opportunities for teacher learning, including a focus on a specific content area, clear connections to the classroom and the curriculum being taught, and sustained support over time (National Research Council, 2007b). The research indicates that superficial coverage of topics that are unrelated to school priorities or to teaching practice, with little or no follow-up to support classroom implementation, are of limited value (DeSimone et al., 2002; Garet et al., 1999). Instead, sustained engagement with teachers over an extended period of weeks or months is required to effect lasting change in instruction and strengthen teachers' confidence in their knowledge and teaching of science content (Rosenberg, Heck, and Banilower, 2005; Supovitz and Turner, 2000).

NASA pursues a wide variety of projects and activities aimed at teacher support and professional development. NASA defines their professional development offerings as either of short or long duration. Short-duration activities are events for inservice educators that last less than 2 days. Long-duration activities last longer than 2 days or are offered over an extended period of time. The short-duration events are intended to meet the objective of engaging teachers, while the long-duration events are intended to meet the more demanding objective of educating teachers.

A recent inventory of NASA's education portfolio (Schwerin, 2006) catalogued 150 professional development activities for K-12 teachers across the headquarters Office of Education, the mission directorates and the centers. Of these, 53 percent (80 activities) were short duration as defined by NASA and 47 percent (70 activities) were long duration as defined by NASA. In the headquarters Office of Education, 13 percent (3 activities) were short duration and 87 percent (21 activities) were long duration. In the mission directorates and centers, 61 percent (77 activities) were short duration and 39 percent (49 activities) were long duration.

Although the research evidence cited above calls into question the utility of short-term professional development, it is important to consider the purpose of a professional development opportunity when assessing the design. If an opportunity is intended merely to make teachers aware of

NASA resources and briefly acquaint them with what is available, a short-term program may be appropriate. However, it is inappropriate to label such an activity as a professional development program; rather, it should be called an informational meeting or some similar name.

For activities that NASA defines as long duration, there is a different concern. The time for those activities is not commensurate with the extended engagement needed to support change in teacher practice: much of the "long-duration" activities with teachers should more properly labeled as intermediate in length.

SEVEN CORE EDUCATION PROJECTS

This section presents our analysis of the seven core projects in the Office of Education Elementary and Secondary Program, drawing on the framework presented above. For each project, the committee identifies both its strengths and areas for improvement. As a setting for this analysis, a summary of the major goals and intended outcomes (if specified) for each project are presented in Box 4-1.

Aerospace Education Services Project

The Aerospace Education Services Project (AESP), which was established 45 years ago, is designed to provide customized opportunities for showcasing NASA-related curriculum materials and activities in formal and informal settings with educators in the states and U.S. territories. To carry out the program, NASA, through the AESP contractor, employs a corps of aerospace education specialists who are former teachers and are required to have at least 5 years of classroom teaching experience in grades 4 through 12. These specialists are assigned to a NASA center and travel to provide services to the schools or teachers in the designated region. There are currently 23 specialists. Typically, specialists respond to requests for services and programs from interested parties, such as school groups, districts, teachers, or administrators. According to a 2004 evaluation report (Horn and McKinley, 2004), about 62.5 percent of the specialists' time is spent either preparing for or making school-site presentations. The specialists are also responsible for mapping NASA materials against the science and mathematics standards of the states in their region—a map that is intended to inform teachers which activities will help them "meet" a particular standard. The remainder of the time is spent on travel, leave, and personal professional development activities (Horn and McKinley, 2004).

Recently, the project has been significantly revised to provide the infrastructure needed for a newer education effort, the NASA Explorer Schools (NES). Aerospace education specialists are now called on to provide or

BOX 4-1
Goals and Intended Outcomes:
NASA Core K-12 Education Projects

Aerospace Education Services Project (AESP)
Provide customized professional development opportunities that educate inservice and preservice teachers that are aligned to their states' standards, to gain rigorous and relevant content understanding for teaching in the STEM disciplines and how they relate to NASA research and development.
Build the nation's workforce by engaging K-12 students and families in educational opportunities using the NASA mission, the STEM disciplines, and research-based teaching.
Support and nurture state and national partnerships with education agencies, professional organizations, and informal education entities to collaborate STEM literacy and awareness of NASA's mission.
Support family participation in the NASA mission.
Support the NASA Office of Education and NASA pathfinder initiatives to provide compelling experiences for educators and students that increase interest in STEM coursework and careers.

NASA Explorer Schools (NES) (includes the Digital Learning Network [DLN])
Goal 1: Provide all students the opportunity to explore science, technology, engineering, mathematics, and geography.
Goal 2: Provide educators with sustained professional development, unique STEM-based teaching, and collaborative tools.
Goal 3: Build strong family involvement within NES.
Outcome: Increase student knowledge about careers in science, technology, engineering, mathematics, and geography.
Outcome: Increase student ability to apply STEM concepts and skills in meaningful ways.
Outcome: Increase the active participation and professional growth of educators in science.
Outcome: Increase the academic assistance for and technology use by educators in schools with high populations of underserved students.
Outcome: Increase family involvement in children's learning.

Science, Engineering, Mathematics and Aerospace Academy (SEMAA)
Inspire a more diverse student population to pursue careers in STEM-related fields.

Engage students, parents, and teachers by incorporating emerging technologies. Educate students by utilizing rigorous STEM curricula that meet national mathematics, science, and technology standards and encompass the research and technology of NASA's four mission directorates.

Education Flight Projects (EFP)

Develop and provide NASA-unique experiences, opportunities, content, and resources to educators to increase K-12 student interest and achievement in STEM disciplines.

Develop and facilitate a Network of Educator Astronaut Teachers (NEAT)-like group of highly motivated educators.

Build internal and external partnerships with formal and informal education communities to create unique learning opportunities and professional development experiences.

Educator Astronaut Project (EAP)

Develop and provide NASA-unique experiences, opportunities, content, and resources to educators to increase K-12 student interest and achievement in STEM disciplines.

Develop and facilitate a Network of Educator Astronaut Teachers (NEAT)-like group of highly motivated educators.

Build internal and external partnerships with formal and informal education communities to create unique learning opportunities and professional development experiences.

Interdisciplinary National Science Project Incorporating Research and Education Experience (INSPIRE)

Attract and retain students in STEM disciplines.

SOURCE: Information from NASA's 2006 project plans and personal communication, Shelley Canright, outcome manager, Elementary and Secondary and e-Education Programs.

support teacher training or student activities for NES and to support the development and implementation of school "action plans" for the use of NASA units and materials. In fact, specialists report that they now spend about 60 percent of their time working with NES and another 10 percent with the digital learning network (DLN), which is part of NES. The rest of their time is allocated for non-NES schools and teachers (20%) and on NASA center-related programming (10%) (Horn and McKinley, 2006).

Project Evaluations

AESP was the subject of a 3-year external evaluation in 2001–2004 (Horn and McKinley, 2004) and a small follow-up evaluation in 2006 (Horn and McKinley, 2006). In the 3-year evaluation, a variety of methods (surveys, interviews, site visits, presentations, review of documents, and the NASA Education Evaluation and Information System [NEEIS]) were used to gather data from a provider and client group in order to address 19 evaluation questions.

The evaluation concluded that AESP provides good support to NASA projects in raising awareness of the available resources and services. However, many schools and teachers remain unaware of AESP services. In addition, specialists most often engage in activities that generate immediate interest but do not necessarily have long-term effects in terms of education reform and improvement and curriculum enrichment. Although there was enthusiasm from participants for AESP presentations, all respondents indicated that the residual effect of the program is relatively low. The evaluation raised the concern that the project might be limited because of its adherence to an "in-person" presentation model, rather than incorporating more distance learning technology.

The supplementary 2006 evaluation (Horn and McKinley, 2006) used case studies of sites selected as exemplary, surveys, and analysis of NEEIS data to address six evaluation questions. The report provides good insight into activities at these sites, but there is no solid evidence of impact.

The evaluation details AESP's role in supporting other NASA education programs (Horn and McKinley, 2006). Requests by NASA programs for support services from AESP personnel are frequent, and requests also come from schools and educators. In fact, particularly with the extra load of the NES, requests have become so frequent that the aerospace education specialists are not able to deliver all needed services in a face-to-face manner; thus, they have begun to use the DLN to reach schools, particularly the NASA Explorer Schools, through the Internet and videoconferencing.

Project Strengths

One of the strengths of the project is its responsiveness to clients in providing services and other types of support through a network of regionally based specialists. Another is the use of former teachers as the NASA educators. This approach provides a group of knowledgeable former teachers who have some understanding of school systems and of the instructional needs of students. The geographic distribution of these educators allows each AESP specialist to become knowledgeable about the state standards for the two or three states they serve.

The ability of the specialists to engage the regional educational system and form local or regional partnerships is critical for ensuring that NASA's activities are used in an effective way as part of school science and mathematics instruction. The specialists are particularly important in rural states or states without NASA centers that may otherwise have little access to NASA activities and materials.

Areas for Improvement

The distributed model also has a potential weakness. The quality of the services delivered regionally appears to depend heavily on the individual specialists and the relationships a particular specialist is able to build with local educational organizations, districts, and schools. In this respect, a high turnover rate for specialists, which was noted in the 2006 evaluation report, is a problem. In addition, the specialists' role in the NASA Explorer Schools appears to be limiting the amount of time for them to work in other schools (Horn and McKinley, 2006).

The committee is concerned about the ability of specialists to remain abreast of newly emerging NASA science and technology related to NASA missions. A yearly workshop, the current means for updating specialists on new developments, seems insufficient for keeping them truly up to date. Specialists need immediate links to the science, scientists, technology, and engineers in the agency in order to be able to effectively communicate current science and engineering developments and information to teachers and students.

In the committee's view, the stated objectives for the project are too broad, and, therefore, potentially misleading. Those objectives closely follow the overall objectives for the Elementary and Secondary Program, with little specification to make them more appropriate to AESP's scope and target audiences. In addition, the breadth and lack of structure in the project has led to a lack of stability in the focus and sustainability of specific project goals, and there is little evidence of any sustained effects on teachers' professional development. There are some teachers who, by their own testimony, have found the opportunities offered by the program valuable, but this seems to be more the result of good choices by individual dedicated "customers" rather than a consequence of good project design. A system for setting priorities for services might be useful to ensure a broader base of "customers," rather than relying solely on a customer-initiated, first-come, first-served approach (which may serve the same few teachers year after year).

Finally, it appears that the basic design of the project hasn't changed in 40 years and, as noted above, remains structured mainly around personal contact (although with some recent forays into other approaches because of the workload). Personal contact is indeed critical for building relationships and networks; however, NASA should also explore how information and communication technology such as the Internet can be used to disseminate materials, connect to schools, and improve and increase communication in general. Such use of information and communications technology could both leverage and extend the impact of face-to-face sessions.

NASA Explorer Schools

The NASA Explorer Schools (NES), launched in 2003, consist of 3-year partnerships between NASA and selected schools, with a focus on under-served and underrepresented populations in grades 4–9. The project focuses on the whole school. As of 2007, there are 200 schools currently designated as NES. They are in all 50 states, with at least one school in each state. Overall funding is managed at NASA headquarters, but the project is administered through center personnel, particularly the AESP staff and NES teams. Each school team—composed of four or five people including a school administrator and three or four teachers or specialists—works with NASA support to develop and implement a 3-year action plan for how to work with NASA resources to address local challenges in STEM education. By policy, the project and its school-level action plans consider only NASA-developed education materials, and a primary job of the AESP is to inform the teachers about these materials. Consequently, the action plans mainly serve as a catalogue that identifies which NASA materials can best be used in specific classes.

During the 3-year partnerships, the project provides summer professional development workshops for teams of teachers and administrators, as well as ongoing professional development during the school year. Students have opportunities to participate in research, problem solving, and design challenges relating to NASA's missions. Schools receive $17,500 in grants to support the purchase of technology tools, online services, and inservice support for the integration of technology that engages students in STEM learning. Because of the role of the Digital Learning Network in the NES, a significant expenditure is often to bring full videoconferencing capability to each school site.

The NES project itself does not have the funding to provide all of the needed services to NES schools. Many are provided through other NASA K-12 programs, such as AESP or SEMAA, or through other organizations. AESP specialists, for example, work directly with each school and are the most important mechanism for NES team members to receive onsite professional development training; assistance with such special events as family nights; special training with technology tools, such as videoconferencing; remote control of telescopes and robotics; and collaboration with projects that require extensive preparation (e.g., the Reduced Gravity Project).

Project Evaluation

An ambitious evaluation plan for NES, only partly realized, is currently in motion. The initial plan for evaluation used formative evaluation as part of a "design experiment" approach (McGee, Hernandez, and Kirby, 2003). That approach combines project design and evaluation through a series of attempts to address a problem where different hypotheses about how the problem might be solved are tested and modified until the best solution is identified. In addition, an experimental design for summative evaluation was proposed. However, the design experiment approach was not consistently used, and the experimental design for summative evaluation of sites completing the project proved unworkable (Hernandez, McGee, Reese, Kirby, and Martin, 2004a, 2004b). In addition, there were problems with sampling and approach to analysis that undermined the strength of the data and called any interpretations into question (Lawrenz, 2007).

In spite of these drawbacks, the fourth evaluation brief on the project provides some insight into the project; however, it does not provide clear evidence of effectiveness (Davis, Palak, Martin, and Ruberg, 2006). For example, the evaluators identified the following factors that contribute to successful implementations of NES: teamwork of the field center staff; responsiveness to the schools' needs and goals; ongoing communication with the schools; multiple forms of communication (i.e., e-mail, telephone, face-to-face); and frequent visits by the NES field center staff to a school.

The evaluators noted that these factors map closely onto findings from the literature on school improvement which were also identified in a paper commissioned by the committee (Mundry, 2007). In addition, it appears that the project has been most effective when the schools were already engaged in an effective school reform process and thus could delineate their needs and goals in the context of that process. The evaluation at the close of the first year suggests that one of the most difficult elements of the NES approach is supporting school teams to develop strategies for incorporating NASA's materials with clear objectives for learning and teaching in mind.

Teachers' self-report data included in the fourth evaluation brief (Davis et al., 2006) indicate that they have enjoyed the training activities and that their content knowledge and teaching strategies have been influenced by the professional development opportunities. Students' self-report data indicated that the project has had a positive effect on their content knowledge of and interest in STEM subjects. However, no direct observations of instruction or objective measures of teachers' and students' content knowledge were collected. In addition, no comparison groups were used, and project participants were not tracked longitudinally.

Project Strengths

NES is an ambitious project with commendable goals. The focus on disadvantaged students and schools is laudable, though working with such schools adds challenges, as many often lack resources even for basic STEM programs. The NES model recognizes the need for long-term professional development and cooperation between administrators and teachers to achieve meaningful and lasting change. Of the seven core headquarters projects, only NES offers teacher enhancement opportunities that last a week or more. The initial format of these sessions was mostly a series of multiple, short informational sessions about NASA curriculum enhancement resources, but it appears that at least in some regions the project staff have been responding to formative evaluation input. The result has been that more of the offerings in summer 2007 provided in-depth learning opportunities for teachers and work with partners who have the experience needed to deliver such experiences.

Areas for Improvement

Although the project model acknowledges the need for a sustained engagement with teachers in order to change instruction, the committee questions whether the scope of the work required to support NES schools is appropriate for the agency. Does the project model capitalize appropriately on NASA's key strengths and resources? Is a focus on a relatively small number of schools distributed across all states the appropriate way for a federal science agency to try to affect education? Is the project model effective in improving instruction and student learning?

First, the committee notes that NASA's scientists and other personnel do not, in general, have the deep knowledge of education required to undertake whole school improvement. Improving teaching and learning in STEM subjects for a whole school requires a coherent schoolwide approach to science and mathematics curricula, not all of which link directly to NASA's missions. Developing materials on basic science content (not directly related to space science or exploration) for individual schools is not an appropriate activity for NASA. Furthermore, a coherent science program cannot be achieved by simply drawing on existing NASA materials.

Second, NES involves 200 schools, representing less than 1 percent of elementary schools nationwide. Although deep engagement with small numbers of teachers and students can be an effective strategy for some projects in NASA's precollege portfolio, support for basic STEM education that is not obviously connected to NASA's science, engineering, and exploration missions seems well beyond the scope of work in precollege education that is appropriate to the agency.

Third, NES is an expensive project that draws resources from existing NASA programs in ways that are not obvious in the budget. For example, despite high investments, the project does not provide the level and length of support necessary for successful whole school reform (Mundry, 2007). In addition, NES relies heavily on AESP for support, and there is evidence in evaluations that AESP's broader function is being negatively affected by this work by its staff.

Finally, there is no compelling evidence that NES consistently results in improved teaching and learning in participating schools. Some schools affiliated with the NES project showed increased performance, but NES was not the only initiative in place in these schools. In fact, the evaluation results suggest that creating meaningful and comprehensive changes in teaching and learning in STEM subjects was an ongoing challenge for the NES project.

Digital Learning Network

The Digital Learning Network (DLN) has been a component of NES, but the agency is considering making it a stand-alone project. DLN provides videoconferencing and webcasting capabilities to allow teachers and their students to participate in live lectures and demonstrations with NASA personnel. The project began in 2004 with three hub sites (NASA Glenn Research Center in Cleveland, OH; NASA Johnson Space Center in Houston, TX; and NASA Langley Research Center in Hampton, VA).

Two-way audio- and videoconferencing systems that are based on either H.320 or H.323 standards are compatible with DLN. For participation in a webcast, one computer with Internet connectivity and an optional projection device or a computer lab and Internet connectivity are necessary. Student interaction is possible in a chat forum or by e-mail. To use DLN, teachers select from an inventory of topics and schedule a time for participating in a conference. Most events are available only through videoconferencing (though some are also available through a webcast).

Project Evaluation

In the fall of 2005, project staff and an outside evaluator began developing a method for analyzing DLN modules and the effects of the modules on teachers and students. The team developed a content assessment that consisted of multiple choice questions related to the concepts in microgravity covered in the module. They also developed a general rubric that listed the criteria on which to rate modules.

The rubric identifies several dimensions on which to rate modules using a 4-point Likert scale: description of the scheduler, developmental appropriateness, focus question, objectives, national standards, degree of student inquiry, prelesson, videoconference interactivity, videoconference content, videoconference graphics and video, postlesson, assessment, vocabulary, and resources. A module must receive a score of 3 or 4 points in each category in order to be reviewed. The process for revising modules that do not achieve the necessary score was not described in the report. Limited documentation supporting the rubric was presented. The report does not provide adequate information about the reliability or validity of the rubric.

The DLN staff has made an effort to update the list of modules offered through elimination of some modules and creation of new ones. Decisions about what to eliminate were made on the basis of the frequency of requests by teachers, whether presenters were still available to present the module, and the staff's judgment regarding quality.

Project Strengths

DLN has the potential to allow students to interact with NASA scientists and engineers. The project has been expanded to include webcasts and some podcasts, which take better advantage of new information and communications technology. The staff's efforts to update the offerings and develop a review system for modules are commendable and represent an important step toward quality control and continued improvement of the project.

Areas for Improvement

It is important to review and cull the existing modules, but the most recent effort to do so was based on user demand, with only weak standards for assessing the educational merits of the modules. In addition, it is not clear whether the accuracy of the scientific content in the modules was reviewed. Future reviews should focus on the educational merits (effective pedagogy) and also examine the scientific content of the modules. In the long run, a module design process that includes educational expertise and not just the interests of an individual presenter is preferable.

The project should continue to explore ways to expand DLN's offerings to take better advantage of current information and communications technology, with particular attention to maximizing the cost-effectiveness of the project. For example, expanding the project through creation of additional facilities for videoconferencing does not seem as cost effective as expanding the use of webcasts.

Science, Engineering, Mathematics and Aerospace Academy

The Science, Engineering, Mathematics and Aerospace Academy (SEMAA) Project is designed to reach K-12 students who are traditionally underrepresented in STEM careers. SEMAA was initially established as a joint venture between NASA's Glenn Research Center and Cuyahoga Community College (in Ohio). Initially, SEMAA sites were selected by the center without competition; as of fiscal year 2001, however, sites are only added as a result of open competition or a congressional earmark. The most recent request for proposals for SEMAA sites was released in fiscal 2007 and will support three new sites. The long-term plan is to select three new and rotate off three existing SEMAA sites each year. Sites are expected to continue SEMAA operations beyond NASA funding, supported by financial and in-kind contributions provided by other STEM education stakeholders.

SEMAA consists of three major components: NASA K-12 curriculum enhancement activities, family café, and aerospace education laboratories. The programs are run by K-12 certified teachers that the SEMAA contractor employs and trains as instructors. The curriculum enhancement activities are designed to use hands-on, inquiry-based K-12 activities that connect to research from NASA's mission directorates. Because of the history of the project, the content connects most closely to the engineering and exploration activities in the missions and does not encompass research in the Science Mission Directorate. SEMAA students participate in the curriculum enhancement activities for a total of 36 hours each year, (21 hours during the academic year and 15 hours during the summer, with the exception of grades K-2 that participate 27 hours each year). In the original design, and at most sites, this program occurs after school or on Saturdays. One site has chosen to incorporate the activities into the school's regular schedule.

The family café is an interactive forum that provides information and opens a dialogue between families, local education officials, and other community stakeholders. It puts families in touch with local resources and helps them gain an understanding and appreciation of what their children are learning in the classroom. The family café incorporates three forums: family focus groups, family nights, and home-based family initiatives. Family focus groups take place concurrently with the program's academic year student sessions and provide up to 21 hours of participation for parents or adult family members of SEMAA students each year. Family nights, typically 1-3 hours in length, are designed to be fun, learning events that bring SEMAA students and their parents or adult family members together to work on hands-on, STEM-related projects. Home-based family initiatives are hands-on, STEM-focused activities for SEMAA students and their parents or adult family members to work on at home.

An aerospace education laboratory is an electronically enhanced, computerized laboratory that serves as a training facility for preservice and inservice teachers for curriculum enhancement activities. It engages students in real-world challenges, relative to both aeronautics and microgravity scenarios. It houses aerospace hardware and software including an advance flight simulator; a laboratory-grade, research wind tunnel; and a working, short-wave radio receiver and hand-held GPS (global positioning system) for aviation. Costs for a SEMAA site are $375,000 for the first year ($200,000 for setting up an aerospace education laboratory and $175,000 for operations), and $125,000 for the subsequent 2 years. After the initial 3 years, sites are expected to develop partnerships and raise their own money to sustain the work. The 2006 fourth quarter report on the project indicates that just over $1 million financial and in-kind matching funds were raised during the fourth quarter for operations (NASA, 2006c).

Project Evaluation

SEMAA underwent a summative evaluation in 2001 that covered 1992–2001 (Benson, Penick, and Associates, 2001). The evaluation was based on analyses of program documentation and parent surveys. Statistics on participants reported in the fourth quarter report for 2006 indicate that the project is largely reaching the intended audiences: of the 19,069 participants, 74 percent were African American, 6 percent were Hispanic, and 5 percent were Native American; 41 percent were from families with incomes below the poverty line.

On the basis of records of participation, the evaluation concluded that SEMAA is meeting its goals for reaching underrepresented students. Parent surveys indicated that students' interest in science had increased, and they also reported that students' performance in STEM subjects had improved. However, the evaluation did not provide any objective data on students' performance. The evaluators concluded that SEMAA is highly successful. They suggested that the project should develop a plan to conduct long-term tracking. In addition, the evaluation indicated that Hispanic students were underrepresented in the program, chiefly as a consequence of the limited geographical distribution of sites.

Project Strengths

Overall, SEMAA is meeting its goals, well-matched to some of NASA's strengths, of inspiring students in STEM subjects. However, the project model might more appropriately be labeled informal education, rather than formal K-12 education. The project is reaching the intended audiences, and participants, both students and parents, are satisfied with their experiences (Benson, Penick, and Associates, 2001). The family café is a strong component of the project and aligns with research on effective programs for middle school students that suggest family connections are an important part of learning (Westmoreland and Little, 2006). The SEMAA contractor has done an outstanding job in helping sites develop ongoing partnerships and leveraging project funding by raising matching funds.

Areas for Improvement

Participation in SEMAA indicates that it is reaching most of its intended audience, except for the relatively low participation of Hispanic students. Thus, the project needs to consider ways to increase the participation of Hispanic students.

The committee questions whether the aerospace education laboratories use up-to-date technology and whether having one at each SEMAA site is cost effective in terms of the project's intended outcomes. For example, computer simulations might offer an alternative and less expensive flight simulator experience.

The content of the curriculum enhancement activities should connect with research and activities across all four of the mission directorates. Currently, content related to the Science Mission Directorate is not well represented. There does not appear to be a plan to periodically review and update the activities presented in this program, and such updates are needed.

Education Flight Projects

Education Flight Projects (EFP) are a collection of projects targeted to elementary and secondary teachers and students and to informal education organizations and institutions. The projects are intended to offer hands-on experiences for students; they are implemented through the agency's flight platforms such as the international space station and the space shuttle. EFP was officially established in 2003, bringing together several existing projects. Beginning in 2006, EFP was to be overseen by the Teaching from Space Education Office at Johnson Space Center.

Three activities under ELP are linked to the international space station (ISS): EarthKAM, amateur radio on ISS (ARISS), and education downlinks. EarthKAM, established in 1996, enables students and educators to visually investigate and analyze the earth's surface from the unique perspectives of space. It utilizes a digital camera on the international space station, which transmits images of the earth. Students can request images based on their classroom investigations. The EarthKAM camera flew five space shuttle flights and is now on the space station.

ARISS is an organization that was formed to design, build, and operate ham radio equipment on the international space station. It was created in 1996 when delegates from major national radio organizations and from the Radio Amateur Satellite Corporation in eight nations involved with the space station signed a memorandum of understanding. Through ARISS, students gain experience in telecommunications using amateur radio technology to speak directly with the crew of the space station.

Education downlinks, established in 2001 are live, 20-minute, video sessions during which students and educators interact with the crew of a mission as the crew answers questions and performs educational demonstrations. Prior to the event, student participants are expected to study the space station and its onboard science activities and develop questions to ask the crew. Usually, two education downlinks occur each month. The sessions are hosted by people in the formal and informal education communities, NASA centers and education programs, and the space station's international partners. Live in-flight education downlinks, which have one-way video (from the space station) and two-way audio, are broadcast live on NASA Television.

To participate in EarthKAM, ARISS, or the in-flight downlinks, schools must submit a proposal that describes how the EFP activity will be integrated in the classroom and the intended learning outcomes. The proposals are then evaluated on the basis, first, of educational value, and, second, on whether the timing is possible given the flight schedule. These projects have not been widely publicized partly because of their limited capacity. However, EarthKAM has recently increased capacity and is trying to expand its reach to a broader audience. Currently, many of the educators who apply have had previous contact with NASA through AESP, NES, or the centers.

Another part of EFP are suborbital flight platforms, which will provide various opportunities for students to engage in activity-based learning through suggesting projects for the educational rocket initiative, student experimental module-balloons, student experiment module-sonde, FreeSpace, and sounding rockets.

Project Evaluation

EarthKAM was externally evaluated by Education Development Center's Center for Children and Technology in 2006 (Ba and Sosnowy, 2006). The evaluation was intended to examine the project in light of NASA's education goals and provide strategic recommendations for future directions. The evaluation was conducted over 3 months using qualitative methodology to obtain an in-depth understanding of the status of the program implementation and its impact on participants. The evaluators conducted face-to-face and telephone interviews with project staff and participants; conducted a site visit; and reviewed relevant online and print documents and data from the agency's central database for education, NEEIS. The data from the evaluation are limited as only four teachers were interviewed, and the data from NEEIS were not readily available in formats that allowed for data analyses.

The evaluation provides a detailed description of how the project is implemented and includes a set of conclusions and recommendations. The evaluators stress that a mechanism for systematically documenting the program, for both formative and summative evaluation purposes, is needed. They also note a number of potential areas of improvement for the project, including strengthening training for teachers to use the program and website, expanding and updating the curriculum resources available, and improving the reach of the project.

Project Strengths

EFP activities have the potential to provide very powerful experiences that engage students with STEM subjects. First-hand interaction with data, such as the EarthKAM images, and direct conversations with astronauts can also be a mechanism for building insight about the nature of science, engineering, and space exploration. ARISS is likely an exciting project for a small group of ham radio operators across the world, though it cannot be clearly defined as an educational program.

Areas for Improvement

With the possible exception of EarthKAM, EFP activities appear to reach only a small fraction of educational institutions in the United States. Even EarthKAM does not currently serve the maximum number of schools the project can accommodate. This lack of coverage may indicate the need for better dissemination of information about the project. The external evaluation indicates that the partnership with TERC (a nonprofit organization based in Cambridge, MA) to support outreach activities was successful;

however, this effort was hampered by budget cuts in 2006. In contrast with the potential to expand EarthKAM, ARISS opportunities are limited, and there is a rigorous process for reviewing of proposals. Currently, ARISS appears to reach a small audience, many of whom are not in the United States, and few schools are part of this network.

At this time it appears that EFP does not provide enough support for teachers to help them understand how best to use project experiences. It would be useful to have data on how teachers and students use the resources and what steps lead to most effective use.

Educator Astronaut Project

The Educator Astronaut Project (EAP), established in 2003, trains outstanding teachers to become members of the Astronaut Corps. To date, 190 teachers have been identified as the top tier of program applicants, and they have been made members of the Network of Educator Astronaut Teachers (NEAT). Three were selected to receive astronaut training, and the first educator astronaut, Barbara Morgan, participated in a flight in August 2007 before school was in session. Starting in 2006, the EAP is being overseen by the Teaching from Space Education Office at the Johnson Space Center (previously managed by the Office of Education).

The EAP encompasses several activities. Educator astronaut recruitment/ selection activities guide the recruitment of outstanding educators to join the Astronaut Corps. The first recruitment took place in 2004, and the next recruitment may take place in 2008. EAP provides support for the actual flight of an educator astronaut, including the development, planning, integration, and implementation of education activities during the premission, mission, and postmission phases. The educator astronaut is involved in activities at all of these phases.

The premission activities for the August 2007 flight included materials on the website describing the flight and preliminary projects, such as the design of a pennant that will fly on the space shuttle. During the flight, Barbara Morgan participated in three interactive downlinks. Students also had the opportunity to participate in a challenge to design a model of a growth chamber that might be used on the moon. In conjunction with this activity, the shuttle carried an education payload of several million basil seeds. Teachers could request seeds that flew on the shuttle to plant in students' growth chambers. Morgan set up two small chambers on the space station and discussed the design challenge during the downlinks.[1]

---

[1] Personal communication, Cynthia MacArthur and Edward Pritchard, NASA project managers for EAP, June 2007.

NEAT members are expected to serve as NASA education advocates by engaging their schools and communities across the country in the agency's education services and informing them of NASA resources. They participate in a one-time, 2–3 day professional development workshop to provide them with a background for this work. NEAT members are responsible for developing their own local opportunities for sharing NASA information and resources. The Teaching from Space Education Office is planning to review the design of the NEAT in order to determine how to make it more robust and inclusive of other teachers. They are also interested in determining the best approach to selecting teachers to be part of NEAT.[2]

Project Evaluation

EAP has not yet been externally evaluated; it is a high priority for the office that oversees the project.

Project Strengths

EAP has the potential to inspire many students through participation in the education downlinks and the design challenge. NEAT appears to have been formed in response to the strong interest in maintaining a link to NASA expressed by many teacher applicants who were not selected to become astronauts. This was a creative response to the desire to capitalize on valuable public interest and could provide another mechanism for disseminating NASA's materials and information.

Areas for Improvement

In its current form, it is not clear how NEAT will be leveraged to disseminate NASA's materials and information, both generally and in conjunction with flights of educator astronauts. Examining how NEAT members could best be used, or how links to other projects, such as AESP, might be developed, would be useful. Because the project is so new and because the first flight of an educator astronaut took place in summer when schools were not in session, it is impossible to accurately assess the project's impact.

Interdisciplinary National Science Project Incorporating Research and Education Experience

The Interdisciplinary National Science Project Incorporating Research and Education Experience (INSPIRE), which is in a formative stage, is a

---

[2]Personal communication, Cynthia MacArthur and Edward Pritchard, June 2007.

replacement for a former program NASA SHARP. INSPIRE is a three-tiered project designed to maximize student participation and involvement in STEM subjects and to strengthen and enhance the STEM pipeline from middle school through high school and to the undergraduate level. Tier I is junior explorers (grades 9 and 10); tier II is junior guest researchers (grades 11 and 12); and tier III is collegiate interns (rising college freshmen and sophomores). INSPIRE is still in the planning stages; a pilot phase began in summer 2007. INSPIRE is designed to provide critical STEM pathways for eligible students, with special emphasis on underrepresented and underserved groups. Students will be exposed to STEM experiences and encouraged to consider graduate studies in STEM fields. It is also hoped that INSPIRE will provide a public benefit by incorporating parent and community participation through program activities that inform and engage the public in NASA's exploration vision. INSPIRE will offer research experiences, short courses, workshops, and seminars for students.

Project Evaluation

The project is still in the design and planning stages.

Project Strengths

Although INSPIRE is not yet implemented, the committee commissioned a paper to review the research literature on projects designed to engage underrepresented students in STEM subjects and compare best practice to INSPIRE's design. (Hall, 2007) The author concludes that the INSPIRE model mirrors much of best practice about teaching and learning STEM subjects in out-of-school time, including such program elements as mentoring, family involvement, inquiry-based learning, and hands-on activities.

Areas for Improvement

Hall (2007) also provides suggestions to move the design closer to best practice. The author encourages the incorporation of hands-on activities and suggests that INSPIRE make use of existing informal education organizations, such as Boys and Girls Clubs and faith-based organizations. For example, INSPIRE might use youth organization staff as cofacilitators, adapting effective procedures from youth organizations and creating similar learning environments or spaces that have proven successful for those organizations. The author particularly cautions against activities in INSPIRE that might too closely resemble more formal school learning experiences. Rather, activities should be delivered in a way that provides youth with opportunities for choice, independence, flexibility, and social experiences.

Finally, the author points out that INSPIRE staff might consider calling on high school guidance staff and science educators to refer students who might otherwise be overlooked as INSPIRE candidates because they are not motivated by STEM subjects as taught in traditional classrooms.

CROSS-CUTTING ISSUES

Through the committee's analyses of the seven core projects, three cross-cutting issues emerged: improving the process for program and project design and improvement; drawing on outside expertise in education; and maintaining a connection to the science and engineering in the agency. It is not the committee's intent to imply that NASA gives no attention to these issues: each of them is discussed in NASA's new strategic plan for education. Rather, the committee seeks to emphasize the importance of these issues as a means to improve and bring more coherence to the agency's work in precollege STEM education.

Improving the Process for Project Design and Improvement

One of the most important cross-cutting issues is the need for a more intentional approach to the design and continuous improvement of projects. NASA appears to have already recognized this issue, as evidenced in the emphasis on a portfolio approach in the strategic framework and recent efforts to review projects. Taking a portfolio approach seriously will entail using strategies the agency has not consistently used in the past.

First, the agency might benefit from further articulation of a strategy for K-12 activities across the agency and the role of the Elementary and Secondary Program specifically. Currently, the Elementary and Secondary Program is charged with contributing to outcome 2, "attract and retain students in STEM disciplines through a progression of educational opportunities for students, teachers, and faculty" and is integrated into the "engage" and "educate" categories of the strategic education framework. Both this outcome and the two categories are broad. A more detailed analysis of NASA's assets, the needs of the K-12 system, and research-based strategies for achieving the stated goals for K-12 education in the agency is needed.

Next, NASA needs to sharpen goals and objectives for individual projects so that they better reflect the scope and specific activities of the projects, rather than the broad overall goals of the headquarters Office of Education. As currently stated in the administrative plans for the core projects submitted to the office, the broad goals and objectives of the Elementary and Secondary Program have often been used as a substitute for individual project goals. Moreover, the projects have not consistently attempted to provide project-specific goals and objectives that would be closely aligned with project activities. For example, AESP nominally targets all of the Elementary and Secondary Program objectives and NES targets five of the six; see Table 4-1.

Likewise, a portfolio approach requires thoughtful planning across projects, informed by knowledge of best practice in education. The process should begin with project design, with attention to how projects complement each other and how they capitalize on NASA's strengths. Special attention should be given to the question of when it is appropriate for NASA to take the lead on projects and when it is appropriate to develop partnerships. NASA also needs to have a systematic approach, based on educational value, for determining which projects that originate from centers or

TABLE 4-1 Objectives for Seven Core Education Programs

Objectives	AESP	SEMAA	NES[a]	EFP and EAP	INSPIRE
Provide short-duration professional development to engage teachers	X	X			
Provide long-duration professional development to educate teachers	X	X	X	X	
Provide curricular support resources that • use NASA themes and content to enhance student skills and proficiency in STEM • inform students about STEM career opportunities • communicate information about NASA mission activities	X	X	X		
Student involvement: provide K-12 students with authentic first-hand opportunities to participate in NASA mission activities, thus inspiring interest in STEM disciplines and careers	X	X	X	X	X
Dissemination	X		X		
Coordination	X		X		

NOTES: AESP = Aerospace Education Services Project; SEMAA = Science, Engineering, Mathematics and Aerospace Academy; NES = NASA Explorer Schools; EFP = Education Flight Projects; EAP = Educator Astronaut Project; and INSPIRE = Interdisciplinary National Science Project Incorporating Research and Education Experience.
[a]Includes DLN (Digital Learning Network).

missions contribute to the portfolio and can be supported and when a new project is needed to address an emerging area of interest.

Periodic review of projects in order to evaluate whether they have maintained their focus and are reaching their intended audience is also critical. To this end, there is a need to have a process for continuous project improvement and periodic "culling"—refinement of the portfolio. This culling should be done intentionally, with input from experts in education, and based on data provided by projects and through external evaluations (see Chapter 5). The criteria for culling and refining projects should be carefully developed and should reflect the objectives for the overall portfolio.

One potential challenge for the K-12 education program is to achieve a balance between projects that achieve a broad reach and those that foster deep engagement with the science and engineering content of the agency. The committee agrees that NASA has an important role to play in both sorts of activities. However, the two kinds of projects require very different designs and deployment of resources.

There is also a need to reconsider project design as the needs of the educational community change and particularly as new technology becomes available. For example, AESP and DLN do not appear to capitalize sufficiently on emerging technologies. Programs that were designed around old technology or old approaches need to evolve as educational practice evolves and as new technologies emerge. For example, the emergence of standards-based approaches in STEM education necessitated a response from NASA projects, and AESP, SEMAA, and NES have made efforts to adjust to those new approaches.

In developing projects, it is also important to consider the investment required to accomplish intended goals and whether that level of investment is sustainable across the life of the projects. For example, NES is an expensive project that also draws resources from existing NASA projects in ways that are not obvious in the budget. Despite these high investments, the project still does not provide the levels of funding that are necessary for whole school reform (Mundry, 2007). In addition, NES relies heavily on AESP for support, and there is evidence in evaluations that the broader function of AESP is being negatively affected as a result.

Drawing on Outside Expertise in Education

The design and implementation of NASA's K-12 STEM education programs and projects should be informed by the substantial knowledge base in the cognitive and learning sciences and education. Such expertise is not a typical qualification for agency staff, since NASA is primarily a science and engineering agency. Thus, expertise in education must be intentionally brought into the agency's precollege projects through a variety of means.

Hiring education staff with appropriate expertise is one avenue. An example of this approach is the position of AESP specialist. The use of former teachers provides a qualified group of individuals who understand school systems and the realities of classrooms. The regional distribution of educators allows each AESP educator to become expert in the state standards for two or three states. Yet even these specialists may still lack expertise in curriculum development or professional development strategies, which are not areas of expertise for most classroom teachers.

The committee also identified two other methods for increasing the involvement of individuals with expertise in education: partnerships and expert review. Both of these are already in use in some education projects and might be considered for wider use in the future.

Partnerships

Partnerships are already used in some of NASA's education projects, and cultivation of partnerships and sustainability are part of the overarching philosophy described in the 2006 strategic framework. The former Office of Space Science explicitly called out partnerships as a basic operational principle: "Base all of OSS's E/PO (education and public outreach) efforts on collaborations between the scientific and education communities thereby drawing upon and marrying the appropriate expertise of the two communities" (Rosendahl, Sakimoto, Pertzborn, and Cooper, 2004). This emphasis has been carried forward in the Science Mission Directorate and is reflected in its guide (National Aeronautics and Space Administration, 2006b). One major criterion for education and public outreach grants is partnership sustainability, and the guide emphasizes that projects and activities "require the active involvement of the research team and participation partners with appropriate expertise." This involvement might include expertise in cognition and the learning sciences; design of effective instruction, curricula, and professional development; or evaluation.

Partnerships can be used successfully to accomplish a variety of objectives, including development of curriculum materials, dissemination of materials, and support for professional development. Examples of successful partnerships include the partnership between EarthKAM and TERC to support educational use of images (see above) and a partnership between the SMD forums and Lawrence Hall of Science to develop space science GEMS guides.

In fact in a recent summative evaluation of the education and public outreach effort of the Office of Space Science (Gutbezahl, 2007), several projects were identified as having developed exemplary resources for formal education; those projects included partnerships. See Box 4-2 for descriptions of these and other partnership projects. Similarly, in many

---

BOX 4-2
Examples of High-Quality NASA Partnership
Projects in Education

GEMS Guides. These guides engage students in direct experience and experimentation to introduce essential, standards-based principles and concepts. Clear step-by-step instructions enable all teachers to be successful presenting the activities. GEMS units offer effective, practical, economical, and schedule-friendly ways to provide high-quality science and math learning to all students. Information about GEMS can be found at http://www.lawrencehallofscience.org/gems/aboutgems.html.

Mars Student Imaging Project. Teams of students in grades 5 through college sophomore level work with scientists, mission planners, and educators to image a site on Mars using the visible wavelength camera onboard the Mars Odyssey spacecraft. The curriculum was developed to align with national science education standards and fit with existing science curricula. More information about the Mars Student Imaging Project can be found at http://msip.asu.edu/.

Sun-Earth Day. A series of programs and events occur throughout the year and culminate with a celebration on or near the spring equinox ("Sun-Earth Day"). These programs are supported by a variety of resources, including a website, print resources, and various multimedia products. More information about Sun-Earth Day can be found at http://sunearthday.nasa.gov/.

Modeling the Universe. A suite of hands-on activities and inquiries is related to current models for the origins and evolution of the universe. These activities are shared with 8th–12th grade teachers at workshops at which the teachers receive content and pedagogical training, as well as classroom-ready materials supporting each activity. After completing the workshop, teachers have access to a webpage and wiki, which contain additional materials and support. More information about Modeling the Universe can be found at http://cfa-www.harvard.edu/seuforum/mtu/.

NOTE: All the websites cited were current as of November 2007.

---

cases, the NASA materials and activities that the committee judges as having the highest quality were those developed in the context of partnerships between NASA scientists and other personnel and existing educational organizations.

Developing partnerships is also a strength of the AESP specialists. The ability of these specialists to engage the educational system and form local partnerships is important for ensuring that NASA's activities are used in an effective way as part of school science and mathematics instruction.

Use of partnerships does not seem to be consistent across headquarters Office of Education projects, nor is it clear that there are consistent methods for determining which partners are most appropriate or have the best fit in terms of expertise for a given project. For AESP specialists, the extent of partnerships appears to depend very much on the characteristics of the individual and the relationships he or she is able to build with local educational organizations, districts, and schools. In this respect, a high turnover rate for specialists, which was noted in an external evaluation of the project, is a problem.

Partnerships can be particularly useful in the design of curriculum materials, but they are not consistently used by individual projects such as DLN and NES. Without partnerships and careful design, curriculum support resources are often ineffective and difficult to integrate with existing curricula. This concern was echoed in testimony provided on May 15, 2007, to the House Subcommittee on Research and Science Education by George Nelson, director of Science, Mathematics, and Technology Education at Western Washington University and a former astronaut. In answer to a question about how lack of coordination might hinder federal agencies from making an impact, Nelson noted: "There is a huge inventory of poorly designed and under-evaluated mission-related curriculum (posters, lesson plans and associated professional development) rarely used in classrooms and with no natural home in a coherent standards-based curriculum." Nelson did identify the GEMS guides as exemplary.

NASA has not consistently tapped partners for expertise in the design and planning of projects. This is perhaps the most critical time for partnerships. NASA should explore mechanisms to bring in this expertise early. NASA should consider which kinds of projects the agency is well positioned to initiate and which projects are better suited to partnership in which the agency plays a value-added role.

Finally, projects designed to develop students' interest in and knowledge of engineering might be of particular value because engineering does not usually receive attention in the K-12 curriculum. The agency could seek out partners and resources to leverage its contributions in this area.

Expert Review

Peer-reviewed competition and expert review is another mechanism by which expertise in education can be brought to bear on projects and programs. Again, tapping outside expertise was an operating principle for the Office of Space Science: "Use outside advice from the scientific, educational, and minority communities in the planning, development, implementation, and assessment of all our education and outreach activities" (Rosendahl et al., 2004). Expertise can play a role on several levels. In competitions, expert panels provide an important filter for determining which proposals have the most educational merit. Expert review of curriculum materials or project design is another mechanism for maintaining quality (see Chapter 5 for a discussion of expertise in evaluation).

It is not clear whether expert review is consistently used in the seven core projects reviewed by the committee. In mission competitions in the SMD, the basic design of a project is part of what is evaluated in the competition. However, the current projects in the headquarters Office of Education were not selected through a competitive process and were not subjected to a rigorous expert review.

The projects themselves also do not consistently use expert review by educators or by knowledgeable scientists and engineers in the design of their activities and materials. For example, the menu of modules provided through DLN has not undergone review by outside experts. It also appears that curriculum materials developed by SEMAA and by NES do not consistently undergo any kind of external review.

The headquarters Office of Education is in the process of developing a mechanism for expert review of curriculum support materials. Currently, NASA produces a number of curriculum support materials that incorporate a variety of instructional activities for students, as evidenced in the large catalogues listing available materials.[3] The current formal review process was developed by the Office of Earth Science and adapted by the Office of Space Science and is now coordinated by the Science Mission Directorate. The review is based on the assumption that materials have been field tested and have undergone formative evaluation prior to submission for review. The review is based on relevance to NASA's mission and education goals, scientific accuracy, educational value (pedagogy), effectiveness of presentation, documentation, ease of use, and power to engage and/or inspire the target audience. Products are reviewed by a panel of five to seven experts, including classroom teachers, education specialists, informal educators, and scientists. The reviews are conducted under contract by the Institute for Global Environmental Strategies (IGES), a nonprofit education organization. Reviews occur on a twice yearly cycle, in May–August, and December–March.

The headquarters Office of Education is currently studying the feasibility of a more frequent, rolling schedule for reviews, due in part to the demands that arise from increasing use of Internet and web-based activities.

---

[3]See, for example: for space science educators, http://www.nasa.gov/audience/foreducators/index.html; for NASA Central Operation of Resources for Educators, http://education.nasa.gov/edprograms/core/home/index.html; and for NASA Space Science Education Resource Directory, <http://teachspacescience.stsci.edu/cgi-bin/ssrtop.plex>.

The process is being tested in collaboration with the Exploration System Mission Directorate and the Space Operations Mission Directorate.

Given the challenge of designing effective curriculum resources, use of a review system is necessary to ensure the quality of materials. Furthermore, in conjunction with expansion of the current system, it would be worthwhile to consider developing a mechanism for culling existing materials that may not have originally undergone rigorous review.

As part of a review system, NASA needs a set of criteria for determining the kinds of topics or learning goals that are most appropriate to develop. For example, the committee agrees with the SMD guidelines (which in turn originated with the Office of Space Science) that it is not appropriate for NASA to develop materials that target basic concepts in science and mathematics that are not clearly tied to the science and engineering in the agency.

One activity that might warrant more attention by the agency is the development and dissemination of materials and activities that offer students and teachers an opportunity for first-hand experience with the processes of science and engineering design. Emerging research on how to design effective laboratory experiences of this sort indicate that they should: have clear learning outcomes in mind; be thoughtfully sequenced into the flow of instruction; integrate learning science content with learning about the processes of science; and incorporate ongoing student reflection and discussion (National Research Council, 2006).

Connection to Science and Engineering Work in NASA

The third cross-cutting issue the committee identified was the importance of consistently connecting NASA's work in precollege education to the science, engineering, and exploration carried out by the agency. The committee recognizes, however, that maintaining this focus in all of NASA's K-12 activities presents challenges for those projects not directly linked to science or engineering missions.

One such challenge is how to keep education field staff, such as the AESP specialists, SEMAA staff, or educator astronauts, apprised of NASA's current work and related education resources. AESP makes an effort to update staff through yearly workshops, but the committee does not believe that this is sufficient. In addition, solid knowledge of the underlying science and engineering concepts is critical for the staff, and it is unclear how this depth of content knowledge is maintained. The use of the Internet and other technology to facilitate ongoing professional development might be one way to help address this challenge.

A second challenge is how to respond to demands from partnering schools to provide more support for basic science and mathematics that are not necessarily linked to space science. There is evidence of this kind of pressure from schools in both NES and SEMAA. In such cases, NASA needs to be judicious in how to respond. For example, developing very general units on forces and motion or on ratio and proportion that are only superficially tied to the agency's science and engineering activities through choice of examples is inappropriate. However, even when development might be tied directly to NASA-related experiences, such as the process of designing a spacecraft, partnerships should be used, and schools should be referred to other individuals or organizations who can more appropriately work with the demands of the general K-12 STEM curriculum. This is admittedly a difficult line to walk; however, in the context of limited resources for education at NASA, it is important to figure out how to do so.

5

Program Evaluation

In this chapter we examine the Office of Education's approach to program and project review and evaluation. Evaluation of its K-12 education activities is the mechanism NASA can use to determine the extent to which the Elementary and Secondary Program is meeting its goals. This determination is critical not only because there is a need for accountability regarding the expenditure of government funds, but also because there is a need for ongoing program improvement. Program and project evaluation can answer questions about whether projects are advancing scientific and mathematical literacy; motivating young people's interest in science, technology, engineering, and mathematics (STEM) subjects; increasing students' knowledge of STEM content; and encouraging young people, especially those from groups that are underrepresented in STEM fields, to become familiar with and pursue STEM careers.

Evaluation of NASA's K-12 education program and its related projects is challenging and requires significant resources and expertise in evaluation. The program goals are broad, and the projects are diverse in their scope and design. The goal of engaging students in STEM activities is particularly challenging for evaluation because "engagement" is difficult to measure, and it requires tracking over time. In addition, NASA's K-12 education projects, in an attempt to address local or regional issues, often vary from location to location, and evaluation design must take that variation into account. Finally, due to the wide range of experiences and activities that teachers and students bring to and participate in at school and in their everyday lives, the specific effect of NASA's programs, particularly short-term programs, may be difficult to determine.

This chapter is not intended to provide step-by-step guidance on how to conduct evaluations. Rather, we describe major stages in the evaluation process and discuss how NASA could improve its efforts related to each of those stages. Following an initial discussion of evaluation issues with some reference to NASA, the chapter is organized by the major components involved in evaluating programs, from design to evaluation of impact. The chapter draws in part on a paper the committee commissioned by Frances Lawrenz to review a set of ten external evaluations of NASA's K-12 projects, including the Aerospace Education Services Project (AESP), NASA Explorer Schools (NES), a module of the Digital Learning Network (DLN), and EarthKAM (Lawrenz, 2007). Lawrenz also reviewed evaluations of two programs that are outside the headquarters Office of Education: GLOBE and the Sun-Earth Day event. Table 5-1 summarizes key aspects of the evaluations, including the questions and the design or methods.

ISSUES IN EVALUATION

The evaluation of education programs is a well-codified practice. There is a professional organization of evaluators, several related journals, and a code of ethics. There are established methods for framing evaluation questions; for hypothesizing the theories of change or of action by which a program expects to reach its goals; for developing measures of the extent to which the stages of a theory are realized; and for crafting an evaluation design, collecting data, analyzing the data, and reaching conclusions about the import of the investigation. Although there are disputes in the field about such issues as the best design to use for particular kinds of questions, the practices are widely understood and accepted.

In carrying out a specific program evaluation, it is important to be clear about the intended goals and objectives of a program, as well as to distinguish the purposes of the evaluation itself, in order to frame questions appropriately and design the evaluation to address those questions. The key to an effective evaluation is a design that answers the specific questions that are relevant for decisions at a given time. Sometimes, quantitative data may be necessary; at other times rich qualitative data are more responsive to the specific questions.

One way to arrive at priority questions for an evaluation is to consider the major audience for the evaluation and how the results from the evaluation will be used. It is important to recognize that one evaluation by itself may not be able to provide the necessary information to meet the needs of different audiences or the decision at hand. For example, program or project developers might want information on how to improve a program; congressional aides might want to know if the program improves student

TABLE 5-1 Descriptions of Reports from External Evaluations of the Core Projects

Program	Report Title	Evaluation Questions/Focus	Type of Data
NASA Explorer Schools	Brief 1—Evaluation Framework: Evaluating the Quality and Impact of the NASA Explorer Schools Program (McGee, Hernandez, and Kirby, 2003)	Plan for a design experiment and a comparative study.	No data available.
NASA Explorer Schools	Brief 2—A Program in the Making: Evidence from Summer 2003 Workshops (Hernandez et al., 2004)	• What is the profile of schools designated as NASA Explorer Schools? • What are the top target standards of selected schools? • What are the participants' perspectives and beliefs about teaching, learning, and technology? • Who participated in the summer 2003 workshops and what did they do? • What was the participants' feedback on summer workshops?	Surveys and review of applications and workshop agendas.
NASA Explorer Schools	Brief 3—A Program in the Making: Year 1 Annual Report (Hernandez et al., 2004)	• What is the contextual background/conditions of participating schools? • How did the school teams organize to meet their goals? • How did school teams' strategic planning approaches work? • What is the quality of professional development supports? • How did overall NES program guidelines/supports facilitate participation? • What is the impact of program participation at end of year 1?	Use of existing data, surveys of participants, focus groups of participants and program personnel.

NASA Explorer Schools	Brief 4—Evidence That the Model is Working (Davis, Palak, Martin, and Ruberg, 2006)	• How is the NES model being implemented? • How does NES encourage more involvement with NASA program products and services? • How does NASA involvement increase teacher professional growth? • What is the effect of the program on school administrators? • What is the effect of the program on family/caregiver involvement? • What is the effect of the program on students' interest, career aspirations, and knowledge of science, technology, engineering, mathematics, and geography?	Several different data gathering methods were used from three main perspectives: NASA personnel, schools, and students and families. Methods included surveys, content assessments, interviews, observations, document analyses, and interactions.
NASA Explorer Schools	Evaluation Plan 2006-2007 (Paragon TEC, 2006)	• Overall Question: What is the relationship of the nature and extent of a school's involvement to their success in developing teachers' competence in using NASA STEM-G resources and student interest, attitude and achievement in STEM-G? • What is the nature of an NES school's use of NASA resources? • What is the extent of an NES school's use of NASA resources? • In what ways and to what extent do the short-duration professional development activities associated with being a NASA Explorer School affect teachers' confidence, competence, and use of NASA for STEM-G instruction? • In what ways and to what extent do the long-duration professional development activities associated with being a NASA Explorer School affect teachers' confidence, competence and use of NASA for STEM-G instruction? • In what ways does NES involvement affect family involvement? • To what extent does NES involvement affect family involvement? • To what extent does NES involvement affect student interest in STEM-G topics? • To what extent does NES involvement affect student attitude toward STEM-G careers?	Data not yet available; proposed NEEIS data and other surveys of teachers and students; student content tests for selected students; surveys of staff.

continued

TABLE 5-1 Continued

Program	Report Title	Evaluation Questions/Focus	Type of Data
NASA International Space Station EarthKAM Program	NASA International Space Station EarthKAM Program Evaluation Report (Ba and Sosnowy, 2006)	To evaluate the program against the NASA educational goals and provide strategic recommendations for future directions.	Interviews of project staff and participants; use of NEEIS data; site visit to UCSD.
Digital Learning Network (DLN)	Digital Learning Network Evaluation Tool Development Reduced Gravity Module (Davis, Davey, Manzer, and Peterson, 2006)	• Develop an assessment device for the reduced gravity module. • Develop a rubric for assessing the quality of DLN modules with extended definitions.	Content assessment test.
Aerospace Education Services Project (AESP)	Evaluation of the NASA Aerospace Education Services Project (Horn and McKinley, 2004)	There are 19 evaluation questions addressing the following 5 areas: • program design and management. • support of systemic improvement. • teacher preparation and enhancement programs that support systemic reform. • student support. • curriculum and dissemination.	Delphi survey, surveys of specialists and telephone interviews with center staff, AESP State Impact Survey, face-to-face interviews with AESP and center staff, site visits document review, NEEIS data.

| AESP | The Final Report of a Study of the Aerospace Education Services Project (AESP) Role and Impact Among Selected Partners (Horn and McKinley, 2006) | • With whom does AESP cooperate and support for delivery of NASA programs to students, teachers, and others?
• What is the form and nature of this cooperation and delivery of services?
• How effective is AESP in its provision of support services for its NASA and non-NASA partners?
• How do these cooperative actions and provision of services to other NASA partners impact on the traditional role of AESP?
• What are the elements or activities of AESP that contribute most to NASA's major education goals?
• What are some exemplary cases in which AESP specialists' work has impact? | Site case studies, surveys, NEEIS data. |

NOTES: STEM-G = Science, technology, engineering, mathematics, and geography; NEEIS = NASA Education Evaluation Information System.

achievement and contributes to the national scientific effort; and high-level NASA administrators may want to know that the educational programs are consistent with the agency's overall goals. Evaluators need to consider which types of questions would be most relevant and produce the most useful outcomes by discussing the evaluation with the various audiences and establishing priorities. Resources will always be limited, and how the data are likely to be used should affect the basic questions and design.

Broadly speaking, there are three sequential, overlapping stages in program evaluation:

1. evaluation for purposes of developing a program;
2. evaluation to find out how a program has been implemented in a number of settings, including adherence to the original design or effective local adaptation (formative evaluation); and
3. evaluation of the effects (impact) of the program, both short and long term (summative evaluation).

As an evaluation proceeds through these stages, it generally progresses from a situation in which a close connection between the program developer or implementer and the evaluator is necessary, to one in which a distinct separation between the program evaluator and the program itself is important. In most cases, an impact evaluation should be carried out by an individual or organization external to a program's administration.

An Evaluation Plan

An overall evaluation plan is needed to address how well a program as a whole is achieving its stated goals and objectives. Such a plan must be based on focused evaluation of the outcomes of individual projects. With appropriate analysis, the individual project evaluations can show how well overall goals are being achieved. Currently, the NASA Office of Education lacks an overall evaluation plan for the K-12 education program and its projects.

Given resource constraints, evaluations of individual projects can be scheduled on a cyclical basis, with high priority given to projects intended to have the greatest impact on student engagement and learning and to projects that face important questions about activities, participants, staffing, funding, or organization. Both formative and outcome evaluations can usually be scheduled in advance. For example, reports about program effectiveness may be scheduled on a periodic basis: staff can plan for outcome evaluations in advance over a 4–5 year period, rotating the projects in the portfolio.

On occasion, questions may arise unexpectedly, and an evaluation would be useful in answering these questions. For example, during the development of a new program, early experience may suggest that the target audience is not engaged. Evaluation may help to answer whether the wrong age group is being addressed, the wrong materials are being used, the nature of the pedagogy is inappropriate, or the activities are already being provided from other sources. An evaluation plan would also outline the mechanisms by which evaluation results can be communicated to decision makers and help to inform project implementation.

Lawrenz's (2007) review of existing external evaluations suggests such mechanisms are currently absent in NASA. It appears that few, if any, of NASA's decisions about the agency's education programs have been based on evaluation reports. Lawrenz speculates that the evaluations may not have provided the information needed to make decisions or that the political environment may move more rapidly than the evaluation environment, and perhaps the reports were not available when decisions were made. Factors like these need to be taken into account when developing an evaluation plan.

Currently, the overall Elementary and Secondary Program is periodically reviewed, but it has not undergone a true external evaluation. Moreover, the timing of external evaluations of individual projects appears to have been determined by individual project officers with little strategic coordination across the program. This situation does appear to be changing. There is a plan for evaluation in the Strategic Framework for Education (National Aeronautics and Space Administration, 2006a). In testimony before the House Subcommittee on Research and Science Education of the Committee on Science and Technology on June 6, 2007, Joyce Winterton, the assistant administrator for education at NASA, acknowledged the need for program and project evaluation and outlined the steps NASA has taken to address evaluation (Winterton, 2007):

> The Agency's many Education initiatives have not been evaluated in a comprehensive, rigorous manner to indicate how well all of our programs are performing in support of our outcome goals. We are committed, however, to enhancing and improving our evaluation procedures. The Agency has taken several major steps to improve the evaluation function by: (a) incorporating a detailed evaluation plan into its Education Strategy Framework; (b) defining an enhanced set of outcome-based performance measures; articulating specific roles and responsibilities to ensure accountability; and, (c) allocating the resources necessary to support rigorous evaluations and the overall evaluation function.

Costs

Evaluation, especially evaluation of impact, can be expensive. Past headquarters Office of Education budgets for evaluation appear to be relatively small, but it was difficult for the committee to obtain exact figures because evaluation costs are not listed as a separate budget category; rather, they are included in overall project costs. As a result, there is no way to account for the total amount spent on evaluation across projects.

A rule of thumb for evaluating programs is that at least 5 percent of the total budget should be devoted to evaluation: reports from project managers are that this level of funding for evaluation has not been provided. Insufficient funds severely limit the scope and nature of any evaluation. Given limited overall funds, it is critical that NASA develop a plan for allocating the funds that are available for evaluation.

PROGRAM AND PROJECT DESIGN

The evaluation process can and should begin with the initial design of a program or project. For example, once the goals of a proposed program are specified, the agency can describe the theory of action underlying the program design—how the planned activities are expected to lead to the desired outcomes—citing the appropriate evidence that supports particular elements of the program design (Weiss, 2007). As a next step, a "design critique" of a proposed program or project may be appropriate to help improve the design, or in some cases that step will lead to a decision to not go forward if the objectives cannot be met with the proposed design. This kind of design critique is not expensive and requires only modest amounts of time from people who understand both the system that is being targeted for improvement and what has been learned in prior efforts (Weiss, 2007).

It may also be appropriate at the design stage to carry out a planning evaluation in which evaluators are involved to help diagnose and define the condition that a given project is designed to address, to state clearly and precisely the goals of the project, and to review the proposed procedures for obtaining accurate information and for the soundness of the evaluation methods (Rossi and Freeman, 1993; Weiss, 1998). The result can provide a more detailed description of a project, including major goals and objectives, activities, participants, resources, timeline, and intended accomplishments. It can also help to document the state of key outcomes prior to the project in order to provide a baseline for measuring impact.

NASA has begun to build a theory of action in its strategic framework with the pyramid and the push-pull model, described in Chapter 2. This framework and model, however, have very little specificity. More detail about mechanisms and expected effects based on research is needed for individual projects. The model developed as part of the NES evaluation is an example, though it is very detailed and somewhat difficult to use because of its complexity.

As noted in Chapter 4, NASA could improve efforts to subject program and project designs to appropriate analysis. One approach would be to have the program or project design and theory of action and evidence presented in support of the design critiqued by a small number of external experts, perhaps by forming an advisory group, or through soliciting ad hoc reviewers (Weiss, 2007).

Specifying and Measuring Program Outcomes

An important element of project design is the specification of desired outcomes and deciding how those outcomes will be measured. NASA has taken this step at the program level by specifying a set of outputs and outcomes for the major objectives of the K-12 education program as a whole (see Table 5-2). These specifications are important for guiding both internal and external evaluations of the overall program.

Although NASA's specified outputs and outcomes developed for each program objective are appropriate, there are three areas for improvement. First, in some cases, the proposed outcome is not a good representation of the objective: that is, the outcome does not have good face validity as a measure of the objective (Kerlinger and Lee, 2000; Moiser 1947). Second, the proposed outcome is actually difficult or impossible to measure. Third, the data collected for an outcome will be difficult to interpret. The rest of this section discusses NASA's specified objectives, outputs, and outcomes and the areas for improvement; Table 5-2 provides an overview of the objectives, outputs, and outcomes.

Educator Professional Development—Short Duration

The objective for short-term professional development sessions is to engage teachers. The output identified for this objective is the number of teachers participating in a session. The outcome is the number of teachers using "NASA STEM resources" and rating them as effective. Given the limited goal of engagement and the short duration of the session, these measures seem reasonable. However, this sort of measure of output could press NASA to simply offer sessions to more and more teachers, regardless of how effectively they might be turning their engagement into implementing any changes in their teaching. Furthermore, the count of teachers who participated in a session may be difficult to interpret and may make sense only when compared to previous years' enrollment or some other such measure. Finally, given the approximately 2 million teachers in the United States, the number of teachers reached is unlikely to be significant by itself.

The outcomes (use and perceived effectiveness of materials) may also present some difficulties. Use implies that a shift in the science curriculum in

TABLE 5-2 Objectives, Outputs, and Outcomes for the Elementary and Secondary Program

Objective	Output	Outcome
2.1 Educator Professional Development—Short Duration Objective: (**Engage**) Provide short-duration professional development and training opportunities to educators, equipping them with the skills and knowledge to attract and retain students in STEM disciplines.	2.1.1 Number of elementary and secondary educators participating in NASA-sponsored short-term professional development opportunities.	2.1.2 Percentage of elementary and secondary educators using NASA content-based STEM resources in the classroom. 2.1.3 Percentage of elementary and secondary educators using NASA content-based STEM resources in the classroom who rate the resources as effective.
2.2 Educator Professional Development—Long Duration Objective: (**Educate**) Provide long-duration and/or sustained professional development training opportunities to educators that result in deeper content understanding and/or competence and confidence in teaching STEM disciplines.	2.2.1 Number of elementary and secondary educators participating in NASA-sponsored professional development opportunities. 2.2.2 Number of colleges and universities training elementary and secondary educators who partner with NASA in their STEM teacher educator programs.	2.2.3 Number of teachers who use NASA content or resources as a result of another teacher's direct involvement with a NASA program. 2.2.4 Percentage of NASA teacher program participants who become active within a national network to train other teachers. 2.2.5 Percentage of elementary and secondary educators who participate in NASA training programs who use NASA resources in their classroom instruction. 2.2.6 Evidence that teachers who use NASA resources perceive themselves as more effective teachers in achieving STEM results with their students. 2.2.7 Percentage of higher education partners that use NASA resources in STEM preservice education methods courses and student teaching experiences.

2.3 **Curricular Support Resources**
Objective: (**Educate**) Provide curricular support resources that use NASA themes and content to (a) enhance student skills and proficiency in STEM disciplines (**Educate**); (b) inform students about STEM career opportunities (**Engage**); (c) communicate information about NASA's mission activities (**Engage**).

2.3.1 Quantity, type, and cost of educational resources being produced.
2.3.2 Quantity, type, and cost of educational resources approved through the NASA education product review process.
2.3.3 Number of approved materials that are electronically accessible.

2.3.4 Customer satisfaction data regarding relevance of NASA educational resources.
2.3.5 Customer satisfaction data regarding effectiveness of NASA educational resources.

2.4 **Student Involvement K-12**
Objective: (**Engage**) Provide K-12 students with authentic first-hand opportunities to participate in NASA mission activities, thus inspiring interest in STEM disciplines and careers.
Objective: (**Engage**) Provide opportunities for family involvement in K-12 student learning in STEM areas.

2.4.1 Number of elementary and secondary student participants in NASA instructional and enrichment activities.
2.4.2 Number of elementary and secondary student participants in NASA-sponsored extended learning opportunities.
2.4.3 Number of opportunities for family involvement.
2.4.4 Percentage increase in number of elementary and secondary student participants in NASA instructional and enrichment activities.

2.4.5 Activities and investigations result in increased student interest in STEM.
2.4.6 Activities and investigations result in increased student knowledge about careers in STEM.
2.4.7 Family participants will show an increased interest in their student's STEM coursework.
2.4.8 Level of student learning about science and technology resulting from elementary and secondary NASA education programs.
2.4.9 Level of student interest in science and technology careers resulting from elementary and secondary NASA education programs.

SOURCES: NASA Education Program-Outcomes, Objectives, & Measures for Performance Accountability Report (PART) and Performance Measurement Rating Tool (PART) and personal communication, Malcom Phelps, director, Research and Evaluation, NASA Office of Education. These are draft items subject to final approval. Ratings on output 2.4.4, outcome 2.1.2, and outcome 2.2.5 are available at http://www.whitehouse.gov/omb/expectmore/detail/10002310.2007.html [accessed November 2007].

these teachers' classrooms is expected as a result of a relatively short intervention. Given the research summarized in Chapter 4, such a shift is highly unlikely. Many previous evaluations in different fields show that teachers rarely change their classroom practice, especially as a result of low-intensity, outside intervention (DeSimone et al., 2002; Garet et al., 1999). Yet since many of the short-term sessions are requested by teachers or schools already familiar with NASA's resources, it is possible that the teachers are inclined to use the resources even with only short exposure to them.

Moreover, the information about use of the materials may be difficult to interpret as things can change in the time between a brief session and the use of materials in a classroom, and these changes do not necessarily reflect on the quality of the session or the quality of the materials. For example, teachers may not have time in their curriculum to introduce new materials, or they may already have similar materials from other sources.

Educator Professional Development—Long Duration

The objective for long-duration professional development is to educate teachers—to deepen their content knowledge and their competence in the classroom. The output measures are the number of teachers participating and the number of colleges and universities participating. The outcome measures are the number of teachers who use NASA content or resources as a result of another teacher's direct involvement with a NASA program; the percentage of participants who become active in a national network to train other teachers; the percentage of participants who use NASA resources in their classroom instruction; and evidence that teachers who use NASA resources perceive themselves as more effective teachers of STEM subjects.

For this objective, there is a mismatch between three of the outcome measures and the objective. Only one of the outcomes speaks directly to participants' feelings of competence in teaching STEM subjects. Three of the other outcomes deal with the percentage of teachers and colleges and universities that become active in using and further disseminating NASA materials. Moreover, the measure of teachers' competence, although relevant, is based on self-reports. There is no objective measure of teachers' competence or increased knowledge, such as pre- and post-activity assessments of teachers' knowledge or classroom observation of teaching practices by external evaluators.

Furthermore, it would be difficult and costly to collect data on "the number of teachers who use NASA content or resources as a result of another teacher's direct involvement with a NASA program." Similarly, "the percentage of NASA teacher program participants who become active within a national network to train other teachers" is difficult to measure accurately. There is no systematic national network of this kind. Participation would therefore depend largely on local factors and whether teachers have an opportunity to train or coach other teachers. Such wide variation may make it impossible to isolate the role of NASA's intervention in fostering participation.

Curricular Support Resources

The objective for curricular support resources includes both educating and engaging students. In educating students, the intent is to enhance students' skills and proficiency in STEM disciplines. In engaging students, the intent is to inform students about STEM career opportunities and communicate information about NASA's mission activities. The output measures include quantity, type, and costs of materials produced and approved through the NASA review process and the percentage of materials that are accessible electronically. The outcome measures consist of customer satisfaction with the relevance and effectiveness of the materials. Presumably, customers will be asked to rate relevance and effectiveness in terms of students' skills and proficiency in STEM subjects, knowledge of STEM career opportunities, and knowledge of NASA's missions.

Again, there is a mismatch between the outcome measures and the objectives. Although measures of customer satisfaction are important, they are not direct measures of students' interests, proficiency, or knowledge of career opportunities and NASA missions. In addition, the satisfaction measures could be supplemented with measures of how many customers access and use the materials, which is not included.

Student Involvement

In contrast to the curricular support objective discussed above, the stated objective for student involvement is only to engage students. Again, output measures are the number of students and families participating in NASA instructional and enrichment programs. Two outcome measures seek to document students' increased interest and knowledge of STEM careers: one measures families' increased interest in students' STEM coursework; the other measures the level of students' learning about science and technology. The second outcome measure is interesting in that the objective is not targeted at educating, but the outcome documents learning. These outcomes are sensible, but they require systematic surveys and pre- and post-activity assessments. It is not clear how such data would be collected and analyzed and over what time periods.

Measuring learning is not easy. If standardized tests are used, the tests may have only a few items that are specific to the content that NASA covered in its activity. Tests cover broad areas, and NASA curriculum materials are quite specific. Even if NASA input is able to change students' performance on a few test items, a noticeable change in score is unlikely. If tests based on specific NASA curriculum materials are used, they must be developed using standard methodology for constructing tests so that their reliability and validity can be established.

Specifying and Measuring Project Outcomes

In addition to the program-level objectives, outputs, and outcomes, a parallel set of objectives and measures should be developed for each project. These objectives and measures can mirror those for the overall program, but they also need to take into account the specific goals, scope, and target audience of the project. If evaluators are included in the planning stages, they can offer input related to setting those objectives and identifying outputs and outcomes. Such involvement will help to facilitate long-term evaluation of a project.

Lawrenz's (2007) paper suggests that this step might be useful. It notes that the goals for most NASA projects are very broad and that it would be difficult for any project, much less one with limited funding available, to achieve these goals in any depth. It suggests that these issues might be resolved during the evaluation planning stages with careful discussions that would include development of targeted goals for projects that would be more amenable to evaluation

FORMATIVE EVALUATION

The purpose of formative evaluation is to provide feedback on the development of a program or project and its implementation. An overarching formative question is "how is the project operating?" The specific questions focus on how the project is being implemented and may include questions about specific features of a project or program, such as recruitment strategies, participant attributes, materials, and attendance.

Whether NASA is developing a new program or revising an existing program, questions can arise about how well the program is operating in its early phases. Identifying program successes and challenges early in the process can help staff make adjustments that might improve the overall implementation or outcome of the program. Sometimes, a pilot version of a program can be run in the developmental phase, and an evaluator can assist developers as the program takes shape.

Other kinds of questions may surface unexpectedly during a project's early implementation. For example, if a recruitment crisis occurs in several different locations, it may raise questions about teacher receptivity to certain kinds of professional development activities. In such situations, it may be helpful to have a rapid-response evaluation plan in place to study the issue. This type of evaluation will usually involve small-scale studies of limited issues.

More subjective feedback from participants regarding the programs in which they take part is often useful. For example, evaluators can ask participants to rate how much they like and value NASA program activities. Such information is not a real "evaluation" of the programs or activities; rather, it is a measure of their popularity. Nonetheless, it can provide valuable feedback. This type of information can be made part of a common information system. NASA currently gathers much of this type of information, though the information system, NEISS, is flawed (see the section in this chapter on NEISS).

Lawrenz's review of NASA's external evaluations of projects suggests that the headquarters Office of Education is doing an adequate job of formative evaluation. All of the evaluations she reviewed addressed formative questions. They all reported on how the projects were operating and how those operations fit with NASA's larger goals. They all also provided recommendations as to how the projects might be improved or changed. Most also provided a good deal of information about how participants and administrators viewed the projects. In Lawrenz's view, they provided interesting descriptive information about the projects from the perspective of those actually participating in them.

OUTCOME OR EFFECTIVENESS EVALUATION

Determining how well a program or project is achieving its goals and objectives is at the heart of any evaluation process. Data on outcomes are needed to demonstrate a program's strengths and weaknesses, both to the public and to program and project administrators. The data from outcome evaluations are also useful for initiating program or project improvement.

Evaluation of a project's outcomes, also called summative evaluation, can be designed to address several questions. One is to determine whether, and to what extent, a program or project results in the desired outcomes. Another is to determine whether the teacher or student outcomes are the same or different in comparison with the outcomes of other STEM education programs. For the NASA projects, a principal focus of attention in outcome evaluation is the extent to which teachers and students have achieved the attitudes and learning specified in the project's goals and outcomes.

Outcome evaluation can be a flexible process. Evaluators need not limit themselves to just collecting data on outcomes, but can also collect data on characteristics of the program or project in different sites, characteristics of the participants and staff, materials, time, frequency, intensity of exposure, and settings. Using data related to the conditions in and around the program, evaluators can analyze which conditions are associated with different outcomes. For example, does the program have better outcomes for girls or boys? Are outcomes better when the teacher has taken a workshop in space science or technology, or when project materials are introduced in classes daily, or when the school principal supports the NASA intervention? Such data can indicate which features of the project are most desirable under which circumstances and thus help provide guidance for project improvement.

Evaluation Designs

Evaluation of outcomes calls for high standards of research design. In order to know whether the outcomes observed are the result of the intervention and not of other conditions to which participants have been exposed, randomized control-group or comparable comparison group design are desirable. Such designs allow the evaluator to attribute effects specifically to the intervention. Over the past decade, the demand for federal education programs to demonstrate their effectiveness has grown considerably. Policy makers have raised their expectations for program evaluation and now ask for "scientifically based" evidence of impact. Simply documenting the numbers of participants or the geographic dispersion of project sites is not sufficient for demonstrating a program's value (Weiss, 1998). Broadly, the demand for evidence about a program's impact has generated a national debate about appropriate designs for evaluation, and that national debate has major implications for NASA's approach to evaluating its education programs.

Currently, some evaluators and the organizations that fund them advocate randomized clinical trials as the preferred evaluation design (sometimes called the "gold standard" of evaluation). For example, the Academic Competitiveness Council (ACC) report (U.S. Department of Education, 2007a) identifies a hierarchy of designs with randomized clinical trials as the most desirable.

Randomized clinical trials call for the random assignment of some people to the treatment group (people who will be exposed to the program) and some to the control group (people who will not be exposed). Randomization enhances the chances that groups are essentially identical at the outset so that any differences between the groups at the conclusion of the trial can be attributed to the program. Although such a trial is an excellent mechanism for ruling out many rival explanations for differences between groups, it is by no means the only appropriate design for evaluation. When a key question is whether the program people who are exposed to the program attain some specified outcome, a randomized clinical trial is often the method of choice. However, under certain conditions, other methods may be more appropriate for determining impact (for discussions of designs for evaluation and research, see NRC, 2002; Rossi, Lipsey, and Freeman, 2003; Shadish, Cook, and Campbell, 2002; Weiss, 1998).

There are major difficulties to conducting a randomized clinical trial in order to determine a program's impact, especially for the types of programs and projects that NASA supports (see Rossi et al., 2003, and Weiss, 1998, for discussions of the challenges of conducting randomized clinical trials). First, it can be difficult and costly to mount a trial, especially if an intervention is provided over an extended duration or if the impact needs to be studied over a substantial period of time. It is also difficult to mount a clinical trial for projects that are intended to be tailored to local needs and may not have identical features across sites. Second, program managers may be unwilling to randomly assign units (students, teachers, classrooms, schools). Third, participants (students, teachers, or schools) may be unwilling to accept random assignment to a program or control group. Fourth, randomized clinical trials are not foolproof, and studies can be biased even when randomized (Als-Nielsen et al., 2003; House, 2006; Moiser, 1947; Torgerson and Roberts, 1999; Torgerson and Torgerson, 2003). These four issues must all be considered when determining the timing and scope of evaluations that use a randomized clinical design.

Measuring Inspiration and Engagement

As noted in Chapter 2, NASA is particularly well positioned to build on teacher and student interest in STEM subjects. The objectives for the Elementary and Secondary Program and its constituent projects are appropriately focused on this interest, particularly the inspiration and engagement that NASA's programs can generate. Measuring inspiration and engagement, however, is challenging. Students can be expected to offer credible responses—both immediately after a project and over time—about how excited they have become about space science and how much they were inspired to pursue STEM subjects both in and out of school. However, widely used and validated measures of these outcomes are not available.

Engagement may also be measurable in terms of course taking and leisure time behavior. In fact, the metrics developed by the ACC include measures such as the number of Carnegie units earned by high school students in mathematics and science and the percentage of students participating in extracurricular activities in mathematics and science (U.S. Department of Education, 2007a). When these kinds of measures are used, however, it would be valuable to use a control or comparison group of students who were not exposed to the NASA intervention to determine whether it was the NASA input that made the difference in inspiration and engagement.

Longitudinal Studies

Measures of continued engagement require longitudinal studies of students who have participated in NASA programs in order to establish, for example, their enrollment in nonrequired science courses in high school, their majors in undergraduate education, if they undertake graduate study, and even their eventual careers. Even short-term outcomes, such as participation in STEM coursework or other STEM activities, require some follow-up after students have left a project.

Unfortunately, studies that follow students over a period of ten years or more are difficult to carry out, are expensive, and are likely beyond the resources that NASA wants to invest in program evaluation. The challenge, therefore, is to develop meaningful measures for individual projects beyond simply counting participation, while at the same time developing a strategy for determining how well a program is achieving its goals. One possible approach is to mount a large-scale, multiyear evaluation study for the Elementary and Secondary Program as a whole, rather than attempting to do longitudinal studies for individual projects in the program. Alternatively, longitudinal studies might be carried out only for those projects in which tracking individual students is facilitated by the design of the project, such as the proposed INSPIRE project. An evaluation effort of this scale and expense is not appropriate for projects that involve short-term activities with little potential to generate long-term effects.

Current Status of Evaluations

Lawrenz's (2007) review of external evaluations of projects indicates that all of the evaluations she reviewed combined formative and summative elements; however, they were all much stronger on the formative side. Many of the weaknesses she identified make it difficult to draw reliable conclusions about the impact of the projects in question.

For example, the evaluation designs were mostly retrospective and involved only the treatment group and self-report data. On the latter point, much prior research has shown that participants are not always reliable informants. On the former point, the lack of a comparison group makes it virtually impossible to draw any meaningful conclusions about the cause of observed outcomes.

Moreover, the samples of the treatment group were often convenience samples, that is, they came from people who were easy to obtain data from. This approach often involves selecting the best cases, the ones that are easiest to locate, or the ones that are geographically close. As a result, the sample on which the conclusions were based was not representative of the project population. Response rates were often low, and there were few studies that focused on identifying the people who did not respond. Most of the instruments reviewed by Lawrenz appeared to be sound, but little information on the construction of the instruments or indications of their validity was provided. One exception was a student assessment instrument, but the analyses provided showed that it was probably not a particularly strong instrument. There were many instances of case studies and interviews with varying amounts of detail about how they were conducted. There was almost no direct evaluator observation of programs.

There were very few evaluations that actually sought to track changes, with pre- and post-program measures, related to program outcomes. There were several retrospective questions that asked participants to comment on how much they felt they had changed, and most people reported that the programs had affected them very positively. However, this kind of measure is generally unreliable. There were only a few attempts at comparative studies, and these were flawed by selection bias.

In sum, past efforts to evaluate the impact of projects have been seriously flawed. It is difficult, if not impossible, to draw conclusions about a project's effectiveness based on the kinds of evaluations that have been used for most NASA activities. The agency has recognized the need for more rigorous evaluations of impact and is currently developing a plan to do this (Winterton, 2007).

ACCOUNTING AND PROJECT MONITORING

The new plan for the Elementary and Secondary Program specifies accounting and review requirements for individual projects. Project managers are responsible for ensuring continuous input to the NASA Education Evaluation and Information System (NEEIS) for capturing annual data and metrics (National Aeronautics and Space Administration, 2006c). The measures entered into NEEIS generally include counts of participants and participants' subjective evaluation of their experiences. It is not possible in NEEIS to track individual participants over time or from project to project.

The NASA Education Evaluation and Information System

Reports from both outside evaluators and current and former NASA staff indicate NEEIS is cumbersome to use. There are difficulties associated with data entry, data quality, and data extraction.

Data Entry

NEEIS is a highly centralized system. Data entry must be done directly into the central NEEIS website on forms that are slow and cumbersome to use. During times of peak data entry, such as at the end of the fiscal year, the system tends to get overloaded, and it responds very slowly or not at all. In addition, different forms are needed for each type of data entry (e.g., institutional information, individual program managers contact information, and several other aspects of project information). Navigation between the different forms requires navigation of multiple layers of nested menus.

Projects that keep their own data are generally not allowed to transfer the data directly to NEEIS. Instead, the data must be reentered. Projects that want to maintain data that are not in the standard NEEIS forms must have NEEIS staff build custom forms. This can create a bottleneck because the small central team must service the needs of all of NASA's education projects.

Data Quality

There is no quality control over the data entered in NEEIS, nor is there any internal scrubbing of data. There is no attempt at standardization of data elements, such as the names of universities or project managers. If different users enter variants of the same name, the data are treated as if each name represents a separate entity.

Data Extraction

Extracting data from NEEIS can be difficult. Accessing data as it is gathered in standard NEEIS forms is straightforward. However, summarizing data in nonstandard ways requires building a form through a complicated interface or having the central NEEIS staff build such a form. It is not possible to simply extract bulk data that has been entered. In fact, some external evaluators specifically mentioned difficulty with accessing and analyzing data. For example, the evaluators who conducted a recent evaluation of EarthKAM cite NEEIS as a major limitation to their work:

> Another challenge we faced was accessing and using the NEEIS. Learning to use NEEIS was not intuitive and navigating the database was a slow and cumbersome process, which required several steps for each EarthKAM report accessed. These steps slowed the evaluation process and posed a challenge to selecting a representative sample of all the data available. Given the time it takes to access each report, the volume of reports currently available, and the presence of inconsistencies within the data, such a process will undoubtedly pose problems to future efforts to evaluate any NASA program that relies on this system. (Ba and Sosnowy, 2006, p. 6)

The inadequacies of the system were also pointed out in the 2001 evaluation of the Science, Engineering, Mathematics and Aerospace Academy (SEMAA). The evaluators state that, in their judgment, the data in the central database (at the time called EDCATS), offered little of value in the conduct of the SEMAA evaluation (Benson, Penick, and Associates, Inc., 2001). They recommended that the project obtain authorization for the design and utilization of the project's own comprehensive, universal database that is aligned with SEMAA's objectives.

Project Monitoring and Reporting

In addition to entering data into NEEIS, projects are required to submit monthly and annual performance reports, and they are encouraged to submit a weekly activity report. Projects are reviewed quarterly and annually. The annual review is based primarily on written documentation summarizing the goals, objectives, organization, resources, and accomplishments of each project. The results of the annual review are used to develop an improvement plan.

Presumably, the data entered in NEEIS become an integral part of the annual reports. However, the limitations of NEEIS seem likely to hinder the capability of projects to easily summarize data for reports and to use the data in the system to inform project implementation and improvement. One solution might be for individual projects to maintain their own databases, though there are inefficiencies in this model given that projects are required to enter data in NEEIS.

Currently, individual projects appear to vary in terms of whether they maintain databases or other systematic project files outside of NEEIS. For example, NES maintains school plans and other documents in an online format outside of NEEIS. However, the 2001 evaluation of SEMAA indicated that that project did not maintain electronic records that would allow them to track the progress of individual students over time. In order for projects to effectively collect and learn from data, some improvement to NEEIS is essential.

6

Conclusions and Recommendations

This chapter presents the committee's conclusions and recommendations on NASA's overall K-12 science, technology, engineering, and mathematics (STEM) program and on the agency's seven core headquarters projects; it also provides answers to the four specific questions asked in the congressional charge for this study. The committee's conclusions and recommendations are based on the materials and testimony outlined in Chapter 1 and informed by the scientific, engineering, educational, and evaluation expertise of its members. Given the short period available for the study, the complexity of NASA's education and public outreach activities, and the limited evaluative information available, the committee's answers are based primarily on the expertise of its members.

The first section of this chapter deals with strategies for NASA's program in K-12 education. The second section deals with the core projects that were the specific focus of our study. The third section provides recommendations for improving evaluation of programs and projects. The final section presents our answers to the four questions from Congress.

STRATEGIES FOR NASA'S PROGRAM IN K-12 STEM EDUCATION

NASA has a broad mandate to engage in the expansion of human knowledge, as stated in its founding legislation, in subsequent legislation reauthorizing the agency, and as emphasized in its current (2006) strategic education framework. Education and public outreach play a part in fulfilling this mission. Furthermore, as a federal science agency supported with public money, NASA has a responsibility to provide citizens with a return on their investment. For NASA, this responsibility is fulfilled in part by ensuring that the discoveries, knowledge, and information that result from its science, engineering, and exploration programs are effectively shared with the public. One of the ways that this sharing takes place is through NASA's education programs. To successfully implement its mandate in education, NASA needs a clear view of the program's goal and strategies for stability, project goals, and partnerships.

Overarching Program Goal

NASA's role in K-12 STEM education is both motivated and constrained by NASA's overall mission as a science, engineering, and space exploration agency. The National Science Foundation and the U.S. Department of Education share the lead federal roles in K-12 STEM education and are responsible for the primary federal investment in these activities. Thus, NASA, like other federal science agencies, has an important but complementary role in K-12 STEM education. The assets NASA brings to this role come from the agency's contributions in science and technology made through the work in the mission directorates: Science, Aeronautics Research, Exploration Systems, and Space Operations.

Conclusion: The primary strengths and resources that NASA brings to K-12 STEM education are its scientific discoveries, its technology and aeronautical developments, and its space exploration activities, as well as the scientists, engineers, and other technical staff that make up its workforce and the unique excitement generated by flight and space exploration. Because engineering and technology development are subjects that are not well covered in K-12 curricula, projects aimed at inspiring and engaging students in these areas are particularly important.

Recommendation 1 NASA should continue to engage in education activities at the K-12 level, designing its K-12 activities so that they capitalize on NASA's primary strengths and resources, which are found in the mission directorates. These strengths and resources are the agency's scientific discoveries; its technology and aeronautical developments; its space exploration activities; the scientists, engineers, and other technical staff (both internal and external) who carry out NASA's work; and the unique excitement generated by space flight and space exploration.

Recommendation 2 The exciting nature of NASA's mission gives particular value to projects whose primary goal is to inspire and engage students' interest in science and engineering, and NASA's education portfolio should include projects with these goals. Because engineering and technology development are subjects that are not well covered in K-12 curricula, projects aimed at inspiring and engaging students in these areas are particularly important.

Recommendation 3   NASA should provide opportunities for teachers and students to deepen their knowledge about NASA-supported areas of science and the nature of science and engineering through educational activities that engage them with the science and engineering carried out by the mission directorates.

Program Stability

NASA's education and public outreach activities at the K-12 level are broad in scope and varied in regard to the level of effort and involvement. The current portfolio includes projects that originated through different mechanisms and in different places in the agency.

Over the past 5 years, the education priorities and management structure have changed multiple times. For example, in the 13-month period between September 2005 and October 2006, there were four different assistant or acting assistant administrators for education.

NASA's education program has also faced a downward trend in the budget and specifically for K-12 STEM education activities. The reduction in funds is due in part to reductions in budget allocations from Congress as well as redistribution of funds within the agency. The program has also been negatively affected by increases in the number and dollar value of congressional earmarks for projects that have been designated for the headquarters Office of Education without a concomitant increase in budget. These earmarks—from $19 million in fiscal 2005 to $39 million in fiscal 2006—limit the headquarters Office of Education's ability to make judgments about resource allocation that are based on an overall strategy for the Elementary and Secondary Program and on the merits and needs of individual projects. In addition, the percentage of mission funds that must be allocated to education and public outreach in the Science Mission Directorate was recently reduced as the result of an agency-level decision.

Conclusion: Although some projects have existed for many years, NASA's K-12 STEM education portfolio has experienced rapidly shifting priorities, fluctuations in budget, and changes in management structure that have undermined the stability of programs and made evaluation of effectiveness challenging, if not impossible. The increasing number of congressional earmarks has contributed substantially to this problem.

Recommendation 4   NASA should strive to support stability in its education programs, in terms of funding, management structure, and priorities.

Project Goals

NASA's portfolio of K-12 STEM education projects will always face a tension between reaching smaller numbers of teachers and students in a deep and sustained way and reaching relatively large numbers of teachers and students in a less intense or sustained way. As implied in Recommendations 2 and 3, both goals are appropriate for NASA's education program. The challenge is to make sure that a given project is designed with a plan that is realistic for the desired reach and intensity and to maintain an appropriate balance across the portfolio.

The new strategic framework for education represents an effort to bring some order to the agency's overall portfolio. It articulates a set of program goals and objectives toward which all projects should aim. These goals are broad and cannot all be accomplished by any one project. Indeed, they are so broad that they cannot be accomplished by NASA education efforts alone, but need to be viewed as goals towards which NASA's efforts should contribute as part of a national agenda. Currently, in the case of the seven core Office of Education projects, the goals and objectives articulated for each project in the individual project descriptions reflect very closely the overall goals for the entire K-12 STEM education program. This is unrealistic, given the breadth and generality of the overall goals, and may be misleading to both program managers and participants about what any given project can accomplish. For example, long-term professional development is inappropriately defined as anything lasting more than 2 days. Thus, there is a need to better articulate and focus the goals and objectives of individual projects and develop a portfolio of projects that in its entirety achieves the program goals for K-12 STEM education.

Conclusion: Many of the projects within the headquarters Office of Education's K-12 STEM education program do not have clear, realistic, and appropriately defined project-level goals and objectives that reflect the resources available and the target audiences for them.

Recommendation 5   NASA should take a more intentional approach to portfolio development than it has to date so that individual projects are well defined and have clear and realistic goals and objectives given their target audiences. Management of the resulting portfolio should include periodic review of the balance of investment across projects.

Partnerships

Given NASA's primary focus on science, engineering, and technology, the agency employs a large staff with expertise in those areas, while the number of agency staff with primary expertise in education is limited. However, the design and implementation of effective K-12 STEM education projects requires substantial expertise in education, including knowledge of pedagogy, curriculum development, professional development, and evaluation.

NASA's technical staff cannot be expected to have sufficient expertise in K-12 STEM education to allow them to develop effective education projects on their own. Thus, the scientists and engineers in the agency need to work in concert with experts in education, often from outside the agency, in order to achieve the appropriate mix of expertise in science, engineering and education to design and implement effective education projects. Partnerships with educational organizations can also provide a mechanism for leveraging the reach and impact of NASA's projects. The use of partnerships to provide both expertise and mechanisms for dissemination was explicitly supported in the Office of Space Science's approach to education and outreach, and is reflected in the agency's 2006 strategic framework for education.

The K-12 STEM education projects in NASA and in other federal science agencies that the committee found especially promising usually rested on partnerships between agency science and engineering experts and outside experts in education. In space science at NASA, some supplementary curriculum materials were developed in partnerships with the Great Explorations in Math and Science project of the Lawrence Hall of Science; in earth science, outreach for the EarthKAM project was developed in partnership with the Technology in Education Research Center (TERC). These partnerships appear to have been successful. The broker-facilitator and forum model supported through the Office of Space Science successfully supported the use of such partnership approaches to leverage the educational products developed in the missions, as well as facilitating cooperation among different projects with related science goals in developing coordinated educational efforts.

The headquarters Office of Education projects reviewed by the committee do not consistently capitalize on this kind of partnership. For example, there are several existing, successful models of school reform with which NASA Explorer Schools could have partnered to provide resources in STEM education and enhance the reform work through the draw of the NASA "brand," but such partnerships do not appear to have been widely sought. Likewise, DLN modules are generally developed by NASA scientists and engineers and do not appear to involve partnerships with individuals or organizations with expertise in curriculum development. In some cases where NASA education projects have had successful partnerships, these have not been sustained due to changes in management and/or program direction. For example, neither the EarthKAM outreach through TERC, nor an earlier effective partnership with the Council of State Science Supervisors, are currently supported.

Partnerships can leverage NASA's investment in education by ensuring that projects are designed with knowledge of research and best practice in education, aligned to the needs of the constituency the projects intend to serve, and effectively disseminated and integrated in school planning and curricula. For some projects, NASA is appropriate in the lead role, principally for projects that are chiefly aimed at inspiring students or teachers by exposing them to NASA's science and engineering achievements and challenges. Even for these projects, however, design and implementation can be improved by appropriate partnerships.

For other projects, such as school improvement, NASA brings a valuable resource for enhancing student engagement in science, but it can best be used as part of a coordinated school improvement effort, with lead partners who can provide the educational and organizational support and long-term stability that are necessary for such work. The key is to select partners that bring the relevant educational expertise (curriculum development, professional development, pedagogy, district and state school system knowledge, evaluation, etc.) or that are positioned to leverage a project for broad audiences.

Conclusion: NASA scientists and engineers have the expertise to introduce teachers and students to the processes of science and engineering and to the cutting-edge research related to science and engineering activities at NASA. However, to be effective in K-12 STEM education, they need to work in concert with professionals who have specific expertise in education.

Conclusion: Partnerships with educational organizations can provide opportunities to leverage NASA's projects through use of established infrastructures for dissemination.

Conclusion: Examples of projects in NASA's K-12 education portfolio that reflect knowledge of best practice usually involve a partnership between NASA and other individuals or organizations that bring a proven expertise in education.

Conclusion: When designing and implementing programs and projects, NASA has not consistently and strategically built, sustained, and leveraged long-term links with the K-12 education system at the district and state levels, with broader science and mathematics education-related organizations, and with experienced curriculum development, professional development, and evaluation organizations.

Recommendation 6   NASA program and project planning and execution should make better and more consistent use of opportunities to involve education stakeholders, to partner with individuals and organizations that can provide expertise in education, and to connect to the existing infrastructure for K-12 STEM education.

Recommendation 7   NASA's partnerships in education should be designed in light of the specific objectives of each project. NASA can play a lead role in projects intended to inspire and engage students and should use strategic partnerships to leverage the impact of such projects. For projects designed to affect schools, through work with students, teachers, or curriculum materials, NASA should work in partnerships with organizations that complement NASA's science and engineering expertise with education-specific expertise and avenues of dissemination. All partnerships should begin during the early stages of project design.

Role of the Headquarters Office of Education

The scientific and technical work related to missions is undertaken at the NASA centers, affiliated universities and research institutions, and industry contractors. As a result, the scientific and engineering expertise that is closest to the work of the missions is at the centers, with investigators at universities and research institutions, and with mission contractors. Given this pattern, the committee supports the recent shift in management of specific projects to the centers following the 2006 strategic framework and the altering of the role of the headquarters Office of Education to coordination and oversight of the portfolio.

The committee assumes that the specific activities carried out by the headquarters Office of Education will include

- ensuring the sharing of good practices among NASA's education programs and projects;
- supporting information dissemination and shared technology, in part through maintaining a user-friendly and regularly updated website that can enable teachers and students to readily find NASA education projects and materials;
- ensuring adequate data collection and evaluation to assess the quality of the programs delivered;

- acting as a broker among the centers and programs to ensure that excellent educational projects or strategies developed by one center or program are appropriately shared;
- advocating and planning for the inclusion of appropriate educational activities in the programs of the four operating directorates (Space Operations Mission Directorate, Exploration Systems Mission Directorate, Science Mission Directorate, and Aeronautics Research Directorate); and
- coordinating with the efforts of other federal agencies.

Three other roles are critical for the headquarters Office of Education. One is to monitor the balance of the education portfolio and to maintain the appropriate mix of projects. The second is to ensure that education projects are informed by research-based best practice ideas in education and are appropriately evaluated. The third is to ensure that projects leverage the science and engineering expertise of the agency through carefully chosen partnerships. Coordination with the efforts of other federal agencies is also an important role for the headquarters Office of Education.

Recommendation 8 The NASA headquarters Office of Education should focus on leadership and advocacy for inclusion of education activities in the programs of NASA's four operating directorates, quality assurance, internal coordination, and coordination with other agencies and organizations. In the development of new education projects, the office should partner closely with the mission directorates or centers and consult with external education experts.

Use of Information and Communications Technology

The committee found that K-12 STEM education projects were often using information and communications technology that is outdated (see Chapter 4). For example, the Aerospace Education Laboratory used by SEMAA is expensive and may not be the most cost-effective way to achieve the project goals of inspiring and engaging students through NASA's science and engineering. The agency does not have a consistent effort to periodically review project designs to determine whether advances in technology could be exploited to make them more cost efficient or to disseminate them more broadly.

The committee also found that the official NASA website for education is difficult to navigate and does not provide easily accessible and in-depth information about the full range of NASA's K-12 STEM education portfolio. Links to mission-related materials are especially hard to find. Given that the website is the most likely point of entry for many first-time users of NASA's educational materials, a user-friendly and coherent website is particularly important.

Finally, the central database for education, the NASA Education Evaluation Information System (NEEIS), is cumbersome to use and is in need of updating and revision. It has hampered the efforts of external evaluators and likely undermines any project's use of data to inform continuous improvement.

Conclusion: Projects use the information and communications technology that was current at the time of inception; they do not make efforts to periodically update technology. Continued use of outdated technology can lead to inefficiencies in use of project funds.

> **Recommendation 9**   NASA should make better use of current and emerging information and communications technology to provide broader and more user-friendly access to NASA materials, to support NASA's K-12 STEM education activities, to extend the reach of NASA's education activities, and to maintain a centralized data system.

> **Recommendation 10**   NASA should periodically review each project to determine whether its components are the most cost-effective uses of resources, given current information and communications technology alternatives.

CORE PROJECTS OF THE HEADQUARTERS OFFICE OF EDUCATION

This section presents the committee's conclusions and recommendations for three of the seven core projects in the headquarters Office of Education: NASA Explorer Schools (NES); the Aerospace Education Services Project (AESP); and the Science, Engineering, Mathematics and Aerospace Academy (SEMAA). The other four core projects the committee was asked to review are either in early stages of implementation (Educator Astronaut Project), not yet active (INSPIRE), or currently being revised (Education Flight Projects and Digital Learning Network): For this reason, the committee does not consider it appropriate to draw definitive conclusions or make recommendations for these projects.

NASA Explorer Schools

The committee had concerns about the scope of the NASA Explorer Schools (NES) project, given the resources and expertise in education that NASA, acting on its own, can provide to the schools involved. The current model for the NES project shares some features with models for content-specific whole-school reform, such as the use of a school-based leadership or action team to guide the project, the involvement of families in the school community, and building local support. However, NES lacks key features needed for the goal of broad reform, principally use of well-aligned curriculum, instruction, and assessment that are standards based; sustained professional development and teacher learning communities; and focused attention on student learning. In addition, the level of resources that NASA is able to provide to individual schools and the duration of schools' involvement (3 years) are both insufficient for producing deep and lasting changes in STEM instruction. Thus, NES is unlikely to be able to achieve the whole-school curricular reform in STEM education that participating schools are anticipating.

Conclusion: The NASA Explorer Schools project appears to promise support for whole-school STEM reform but does not have the capacity, resources, or duration to do so.

> **Recommendation 11**   The NASA headquarters Office of Education, in collaboration with project managers from the NASA Explorer Schools, should rethink the model for NES given its time, personnel, and budget resources. NASA should not have a leadership role in comprehensive school STEM reform efforts. However, by partnering with other successful reform efforts, NASA can bring valuable additional resources to support and enhance that work.

The Aerospace Education Services Project

The Aerospace Education Services Project is one of the longest running projects in NASA's K-12 STEM education program and has enjoyed an enthusiastic group of supporters who continue to use its services. Recent external evaluations of the project documented the potential strengths of having regional specialists in place to develop ties to local educational organizations. However, the strength of those ties depends on the skills of individual specialists and how long they stay in the positions. The overall effectiveness of the project would likely be improved if it were fully integrated and coordinated with state and local education agencies. The project would also benefit from identifying the reasons for high turnover of specialists and consider ways to achieve greater stability in staffing these positions.

The amount and kind of training provided to specialists also appears to be insufficient. Currently, specialists participate in yearly professional development sessions to update their knowledge of NASA missions. They do not receive support to develop expertise in designing and providing professional development, yet much of their work is in this area. Moreover, the strategy for responding to requests for AESP services appeared to be on a first-come, first-served basis. A more systematic priority system that is designed strategically to reach desired audiences and expand the network of schools and teachers that use NASA's resources is desirable.

Conclusion: AESP specialists need more frequent and more in-depth opportunities to learn about the science and engineering related to the missions, especially because this content can change continuously over the life of a mission. Specialists may also need more support to maintain and update their expertise in education, particularly in areas they may not have had the opportunity to develop as classroom teachers, such as designing and providing professional development for teachers.

> **Recommendation 12**   The AESP project should be designed so as to better integrate and coordinate services with state and local education agencies.

> **Recommendation 13**   Specialists in the Aerospace Education Services Project should receive more intensive and more frequent training to ensure they have sufficient understanding of the science and engineering issues related to the educational products that they are expected to disseminate. They also should receive professional development in aspects of education in which they may not have developed expertise as teachers, such as providing professional development for teachers.

> **Recommendation 14**   The AESP project managers, in collaboration with the NASA Office of Education, should set priorities for providing services to teachers and schools other than doing so on a first-come, first-served basis.

The Science, Engineering, Mathematics and Aerospace Academy

The committee commends SEMAA for its focus on underserved and underrepresented populations of students and on inspiring their interest in science and engineering. The project has developed a number of good strategies for reaching students and their families and has worked hard at raising matching funds to leverage the dollars provided by NASA and to provide ongoing student opportunities at SEMAA sites after NASA funding terminates.

The committee notes two aspects of the project that need attention. First, related to the broad concern about the cost-effective use of technology (see above), the committee questions whether the aerospace education laboratories use up-to-date technology and whether putting a lab at each SEMAA site is cost effective in terms of the project's intended outcomes. For example, the committee thought that computer simulations might offer an alternative and much cheaper flight simulator experience. Second, SEMAA's menu of curriculum enhancement opportunities can better reflect the science and engineering of current missions. To do so would require periodic updating of the project's offerings. In addition, some more systematic follow-up efforts to investigate the longer term impact of SEMAA participation would be valuable for the project.

Conclusion: SEMAA is an excellent project for reaching the intended participants. The use of an after-school project to reach underserved populations and inspire their interest in science and engineering appears to be an effective strategy.

Conclusion: The project's use of technology, particularly the aerospace education laboratories, needs to be reconsidered.

> **Recommendation 15** The SEMAA project manager, in collaboration with NASA headquarters Office of Education, should assess whether the Aerospace Education Laboratory is the most cost-effective way to achieve project goals. The outcome of this assessment should guide revision of the project's model.

> **Recommendation 16** The SEMAA menu of activities should be updated periodically to reflect current NASA science and engineering activity. These updates should be carried out in partnership with organizations that have expertise in curriculum development and with input from agency scientists and engineers.

PROGRAM AND PROJECT EVALUATION

Evaluation is an essential strategy for maintaining an effective portfolio of programs and projects. The challenges of carrying out appropriate evaluations of NASA's K-12 STEM education projects, and of its overall program, are large; most federal science agencies engaged in education are struggling to meet similar challenges. Ideally, evaluation should be an integral part of NASA's education program, incorporating both internal and external mechanisms with varying degrees of formality.

At a fundamental level, successful evaluation entails approaching the portfolio with a critical eye. A "culture of evaluation" would mean that education staff and project managers regularly and systematically review projects with an eye toward continual improvement and that data are gathered with the intent of using them to guide that improvement. In this context, the headquarters Office of Education needs an overall evaluation plan for the K-12 education program and its projects. Such a plan would help to identify the appropriate questions that address program and project goals and outline the mechanisms by which results of evaluation would inform project implementation.

NASA does not have this kind of overall evaluation culture and plan. Evaluations of individual projects have not been done systematically and are of uneven quality. There is little evidence that the results of project evaluations have guided decisions about projects.

The overall evaluation plan needs to address how well the program as a whole is achieving its stated goal to "attract and maintain students in STEM disciplines." Such a plan will necessitate longitudinal studies of samples of students participating in a variety of NASA-based K-12 activities. Such studies are difficult and expensive; NASA may wish to consider whether this need can be served by participation in some more general or cross-agency longitudinal studies of student attitudes to and participation in STEM disciplines. The overall evaluation plan also needs to address questions regarding the outcomes of individual projects. Given resource constraints, external evaluations of individual projects can be scheduled on a cyclical basis, with high priority given to projects intended to have the greatest impact on student engagement and learning and to projects that face important questions about activities, participants, staffing, funding, or organization.

The overall quality of the external evaluations conducted on NASA's K-12 STEM education projects has not been high. As discussed in Chapter 5, these evaluations contained flaws in design, data quality, analysis, and interpretation that undermined confidence in the results. In most cases, NASA had used an external evaluator with the appropriate expertise, but the evaluator was not involved in early data collection decisions and had to work with whatever data had been collected by the projects. Additional mechanisms to draw on expertise in evaluation in education would be appropriate, such as expert review of proposed evaluation plans and data collection at the initiation stage of a project or advisory panels to offer periodic advice on the overall evaluation plan and on evaluations of individual projects.

NASA now collects data on the numbers of K-12 teachers and students participating directly in NASA-sponsored events and on participants' reactions to these events. NASA divides activities for teachers into short- and long-term categories, although the agency does not appear to record actual program length or number of repeat participants. The currently collected data can become part of a NASA information system on its education and public outreach activities and may be useful for project monitoring.

For evaluation purposes, however, data are also needed on the conditions under which the project is conducted, such as characteristics of participants and staff; frequency of activities; materials used; and repeat participants as the basis for analysis that can identify conditions associated with better outcomes or what audiences are actually being served. Such information can help to improve projects and their implementation.

Conclusion: NASA lacks an effective overall plan for evaluation of its K-12 portfolio of projects that includes definition of measurable project goals and objectives, framing of the purposes of evaluations and key questions, and a plan for how information from the evaluations will inform the design and implementation of projects.

Conclusion: Effective project design and management requires that a project's goals, desired outcomes, and evaluation questions be aligned. This was generally not the case for the seven core headquarters Office of Education projects reviewed by the committee.

Conclusion: Data are needed to serve dual purposes: project monitoring and fiscal due diligence, and program evaluation. Current data collection systems are structured primarily for the former. The current system for data collection, NEISS, is difficult to use and focuses mainly on collecting descriptive data such as counts of participants and participant self-reports. Such data are important for monitoring project activities, but are not sufficient for conducting evaluation of the effectiveness of projects.

Conclusion: In recent years many projects have been subject to rapidly changing directives that shifted project goals and activities from year to year. With ongoing changes in focus, it is difficult, if not impossible, to design an evaluation that can capture project impacts across multiple years.

> **Recommendation 17** NASA should develop an overall evaluation plan for its K-12 education program and projects and allocate the resources needed to implement the plan.

Recommendation 18   For portfolio management, the NASA evaluation plan should include some cross-project evaluations as well as project-specific evaluations.

Recommendation 19   NASA should plan the scale, design, and frequency of each project evaluation so that it aligns to the scale and goals of the project and to the nature of the decisions that need to be made.

Recommendation 20   NASA should use evaluation findings to inform project design as well as project improvement. To do so, NASA should establish mechanisms to connect evaluations to program and project decisions.

Recommendation 21   Data and record keeping should be planned to facilitate both project monitoring and evaluation needs.

Recommendation 22   All NASA evaluations should meet professional standards for evaluation. NASA should take advantage of external evaluation expertise to ensure that such standards are met.

ANSWERS TO THE QUESTIONS FROM CONGRESS

These responses draw on the conclusions and recommendations above, as well as on material discussed in detail in the preceding chapters. We wish to note that the timeline of this study did not allow the committee to collect original data on the projects. Rather, we relied on secondary sources such as annual reviews, reports from external evaluations, and data provided by NASA. The committee's conclusions should be interpreted in view of these constraints.

Question 1: What is the effectiveness of the K-12 STEM education program in meeting its defined goals and objectives?

The projects are somewhat effective at raising awareness of the science and engineering of NASA missions and generating students' and teachers' interest in STEM. As presently configured, they cannot be shown to be effective at enhancing learning of STEM content and providing in-depth experiences with the science and engineering of the missions. We also note that there are program elements that do not align with research-based best practice in education (see Chapter 4).

NASA's K-12 STEM education program would be well served if projects consistently drew on expertise in education through partnerships with educational organizations and agencies to guide project development and implementation. We recommend (above) that the headquarters Office of Education adopt an approach to managing the K-12 program that includes periodic review of project implementation and impact, with the intent of revising individual projects or adjusting the balance of projects in the port-folio when necessary.

At NASA, as is the case in other federal science agencies involved in education, few projects have been formally evaluated, and none has been evaluated rigorously. Thus, there are few data across projects on which to base conclusions about effectiveness. NASA does not have a coherent overall plan for evaluation, nor for how to use results of evaluation to inform both overall and project-specific decisions about program design and implementation. All of these factors made it difficult for the committee to form an accurate assessment of the effectiveness of NASA's K-12 educa-tion activities in meeting their high-level goals.

Carrying out a rigorous evaluation of the overall program has been fur-ther complicated at NASA because rapidly shifting priorities, fluctuations in budget, and changes in management structure have undermined the stability of projects and made evaluation of effectiveness virtually impossible. Most of these shifts and fluctuations are due to factors outside of the control of the NASA headquarters Office of Education, including budget reductions, congressional earmarks, and administrator turnover.

Question 2: What is the adequacy of assessment metrics and data collection requirements available for determining the effectiveness of individual projects?

Given that the overarching goals for education at NASA are extremely broad, appropriate metrics are difficult to develop and program effective-ness is difficult to assess. Individual projects have taken on these broad goals rather than developing specific goals and objectives that are appro-priate to the design and scope of each project. This lack of project-specific goals makes it difficult to measure project impact.

Data collection efforts, common to all projects, consist chiefly of counts of sessions offered, numbers of attendees, and immediate feedback from them. This information is insufficient to evaluate the effectiveness of projects or of the program as a whole. Large-scale continuing projects should develop project effectiveness measures. After a program is established, it should undergo periodic outcome evaluation conducted by external evaluators.

The current data collection system, NEISS, is geared more toward accounting and tracking numbers of participants reached than toward evaluation. It does include some measures of participant satisfaction, but it does not collect extensive information related to outcomes. In addition, the current data collection system appears to be cumbersome to use, for both external evaluators and program staff (see Chapter 5). Moreover, project staff do not appear to consistently use data collected by the system to inform the continued improvement of the project. Thus, NEEIS serves a reporting and project-tracking function, but it does not support effective evaluation.

Evaluation of effectiveness is further complicated by the challenge of evaluating projects that focus on inspiration and engagement. NASA has appropriately focused many of its activities on inspiring and engaging students in order to encourage them to become interested in and to pursue careers in science and engineering. These outcomes are perhaps even more difficult to assess than growth in student or teacher learning.

Assessing lasting impact requires long-term records and comparison groups, but no systematic long-term impact records are available for NASA projects, even for those that have existed for a substantial amount of time. Tracking past project participants can be difficult and expensive and likely beyond the capacity of individual projects. In addition, it is unrealistic to expect projects that provide only short-term experiences for teachers or students to maintain such records. Thus, the committee recommends that the headquarters Office of Education consider a program-level longitudinal study that includes participants from those projects intended to have long-term impacts, such as SEMAA and INSPIRE.

Finally, NASA does not have a coherent overall plan for evaluation and for how results of evaluation should inform program and project design and implementation. The external evaluations that were reviewed by the committee were nearly all based on project data collection about and from project participants collected at the time of their participation. In some cases, these evaluations were used to inform ongoing project improvement, but this was not uniformly the case. In addition, the quality of external evaluations was not consistently high: they generally had many shortcomings in their approach to data collection, validity of measures, methods of data collection, sampling procedures, response rates, and analytic methods, and, in some cases, even in interpretation of results.

Question 3: What is the state of the funding priorities in the K-12 education program, including a review of the funding level and trend for each major component of the program, to include an assessment of whether available resources are consistent with meeting identified goals and priorities?

NASA supports K-12 STEM education through funds directly received by the headquarters Office of Education, as well as by mandating that a percentage of funds from individual science missions be designated for education activities. In this way, the agency is demonstrating its strong commitment to supporting STEM education.

Because NASA's K-12 STEM activities originate in different administrative units in the agency, it is difficult to track all of the funding. Funds for the headquarters projects are well documented and come out of the line item budgeted for education. This amount has declined from $230 million in 2003 to $153 million in 2008, and program planning has been significantly affected by an increasing number of earmarks taken out of the education budget. Such funding uncertainties, coupled with management changes, have made it difficult for the agency to maintain a consistent approach and to appropriately match its program elements and their goals to the available funding (see Chapter 2).

For the projects that originate in the headquarters Office of Education, NASA has formulated broad high-level goals that are not always commensurate with the resources of the projects. The intention appears to be that each component of NASA's education program should contribute in working toward these broad goals, as part of a general national effort. In practice, the manner in which this effort has been undertaken in recent years is to concentrate a good fraction of the program's resources on a limited number of schools—those selected as NASA Explorer Schools. For example, the AESP providers, originally intended as a dissemination network to serve a broad audience, have been substantially realigned to provide needed human resources to the NES project. Similarly, the Digital Learning Network (DLN) has been chiefly used as a part of NES.

However, even with the contributions from other projects, NES does not bring sufficient resources, of either financial or human capital, to achieve the type of schoolwide improvement in science and mathematics learning envisaged by the project's goals. The amount budgeted for K-12 education activities, and the human resources in the NASA education projects, are simply not sufficient for NASA, by itself, to undertake a nationally significant initiative focused on systemic improvement in STEM education, nor for engaging in whole-school curriculum reform activities.

With regard to information and communications technology, NASA could make better use of modern information and communications technology to provide broader access to its educational resources and to make efforts to do so more cost effective. The AESP and DLN projects in particular seem well suited to capitalizing on modern information and communications technology. Similarly, the committee recommends that SEMAA evaluate whether the aerospace education laboratories represent current technology and are cost efficient for achieving that project's goals.

A sizable proportion of funding for K-12 STEM education projects in NASA originates in the mission directorates, particularly the Science Mission Directorate (SMD), which had an allocation of about $25 million in 2006. The amount spent on K-12 education programs in SMD is roughly equivalent to total for all projects in the Office of Education. Historically, 1–2 percent of the budgets for science and exploration missions have been allocated to education and public outreach (including undergraduate, graduate, and postdoctoral education, as well as informal education and public information efforts). The recommended amount has been reduced to 0.5 percent, which nonetheless still creates substantial funding for SMD projects because a single mission budget can be as much as hundreds of millions of dollars. The committee was not charged with reviewing SMD's educational activities in detail.

Finally, NASA does not appear to have budgeted sufficient funds for a thorough evaluation of projects. However, the committee was unable to gather systematic information regarding how much has been spent on evaluation because funds for evaluation are not separated in program or project budgets. Nor was the agency able to provide the committee with cost information for the external evaluations conducted in previous years.

Question 4: What is the extent and the effectiveness of coordination and collaboration between NASA and other federal agencies that sponsor science, technology, and mathematics education activities?

NASA has participated in federally coordinated activities, such as the Federal Coordinating Council for Science, Engineering and Technology (FCCSET) and the Academic Competitiveness Council (ACC) and has shared information about the agency's education programs and their impact with these cross-agency groups. NASA has also coordinated with other federal agencies, such as the National Science Foundation, the Department of State, and the National Oceanic and Atmospheric Administration (NOAA) on a small number of education initiatives. However, NASA does not systematically coordinate its activities with other federal agencies or interact with other federal agencies to draw on expertise related to the design of projects. This lack of coordination and collaboration is not unique to NASA. Indeed, the disconnected nature of STEM education activities between federal agencies engaged in such work was identified by the FCCSET panel convened in the mid-1990s, and echoed in the recent report by the ACC.

There have been a limited number of cross-agency projects (generally those based in a specific science mission), in which NASA has demonstrated good collaboration with other agencies. GLOBE is one such example, where NASA, NSF, and the Department of State worked together to establish program goals and contracted with educational experts to develop active earth science learning opportunities related to the earth-observing satellite program. In addition, NASA helped fund the national K-12 standards in both science (the *National Science Education Standards*, National Research Council, 1995) and technology (International Technology Education Association, 2000), in partnership with other federal agencies. When a mission project has cross-agency support (such as the Gamma Ray Large Area Space Telescope, supported by NASA and the Department of Energy), the project-related education and public outreach work has had support from both agencies for a coordinated project. The committee concludes that collaboration between NASA and other agencies on education is most effective when it is driven by shared interests in the science and technology that are the focus of the work.

The committee suggests that consideration be given to developing a mechanism for federal science agencies to exchange knowledge about successful K-12 STEM education efforts. However, although some coordination at the federal level could be valuable, especially in regard to the most effective use of resources, at the project level coordination with state and local education agencies and the relevant national organizations can be equally important. It does not appear that the expertise of such groups is being effectively used either to plan or to implement NASA education programs and projects.

CONCLUDING NOTE

NASA makes significant contributions to K-12 STEM education by providing access to its expertise in science, engineering, technology, and space exploration. It is uniquely positioned to inspire and engage students in STEM subjects and to expose teachers and students to the nature of science and engineering through exposure to the agency's missions. The committee respects NASA's intentions and applauds many aspects of existing projects. However, as our review and evaluation show, the current K-12 STEM education program does not fully take advantage of NASA's unique and valuable educational resources. Steps need to be taken to give the K-12 STEM program and its constituent projects greater impact through sustained partnerships, more effective use of technology, and a culture of ongoing program improvement that includes both internal formative evaluation and periodic external evaluation. The committee's recommendations outline more specifically the steps the agency can take to improve its K-12 STEM education projects.

The K-12 STEM education program in the headquarters Office of Education is to be commended for its efforts to inspire and engage students in science and engineering and to position its projects so that they can best serve students from underrepresented groups. The Science Mission Directorate programs are to be commended for their close integration with the science missions of NASA and for their use of partnerships to bring educational expertise into their work. A balance of both types of work should be continued, and each should learn from the best practices of others both inside and outside the agency.

References

Als-Nielsen, B., Chen, W., Gluud, C., and Kjaergard, L.
2003 Association of funding and conclusions in randomized drug trials. *Journal of the American Medical Association, 290*(7), 921.

Ba, H., and Sosnowy, C.
2006 *NASA international space station EarthKAM program evaluation report.* Unpublished report submitted to the NASA e-Education Department. Center for Children and Technology, Education Development Center, New York, NY.

Banilower, E.R., Boyd, S.E., Pasley, J.D., and Weiss, I.R.
2006 *Lessons from a decade of mathematics and science reform: A capstone report for the local systemic change through teacher enhancement initiative.* Chapel Hill, NC: Horizon Research.

Barron, B.
2006 Interest and self-sustained learning as catalysts of development: A learning ecology perspective. *Human Development, 49,* 193-224.

Benson, Penick, and Associates, Inc.
2001 *Science, Engineering, Mathematics and Aeronautics Academy (SEMAA): Summative evaluation of model, Cuyahoga Community College original site (1993-2001).* Unpublished report prepared for the National Aeronautics and Space Administration, Washington, DC.

BEST—Building Engineering and Science Talent
2004 *A bridge for all: Higher education design principles to broaden participation in science, technology, engineering, and math, building engineering and science talent.* Available: http://www.bestworkforce.org/PDFdocs/BEST_BridgeforAll_HighEdFINAL.pdf [accessed March 2007].

Csikszentmihali, M., Rathunde, K., and Whalen, S.
1993 *Talented teenagers: The roots of success and failure.* New York: Cambridge University Press.

Davis, H., Davey, B., Manzer, R., and Peterson, R.
2006   *Digital learning network evaluation tool development: Reduced gravity module.* Internal evaluation prepared by Technology for Learning Consortium, Inc., for Robert M. Starr, Program Manager, National Aeronautics and Space Administration, Washington, DC.
Davis, H., Palak, D., Martin, J.H., and Ruberg, L.
2006   *NASA explorer schools evaluation brief 4: Evidence that the model is working.* NASA-sponsored report prepared by Classroom of the Future Center for Educational Technologies®, Erma Ora Byrd Center for Educational Technologies®, Wheeling Jesuit University.
DeSimone, L.M., Porter, A.S., Garet, M.S., Yoon, K.S., and Birman, B.
2002   Effects of professional development on teachers' instruction: Results from a three-year longitudinal study. *Educational Evaluation and Policy Analysis, 24(2),* 81-112.
Engle, R.A., and Conant, F.R.
2002   Guiding principles for fostering productive disciplinary engagement: Explaining an emergent argument in a community of learners' classroom. *Cognition and Instruction, 20(4),* 399-483.
Federal Coordinating Council for Science, Engineering and Technology
1993   *The federal investment in science, mathematics, engineering, and technology education: Where now? what next? sourcebook.* Report of the expert panel for the review of federal education programs in science, mathematics, engineering, and technology (ERIC Document Reproduction Service No. ED366502.) Available: http://www.eric.ed.gov/ERICDocs/data/ericdocs2sql/content_storage_01/0000019b/80/15/41/fc.pdf [accessed February 2007].
Garet, M., Birman, B.F., Porter, A.C., DeSimone, L., Herman, R., and Yoon, K.S.
1999   *Designing effective professional development: Lessons from the Eisenhower program.* (Prepared under contract EA97001001 by American Institutes for Research for the U.S. Department of Education Office of the Under Secretary.) Available: http://www.ed.gov/inits/teachers/eisenhower/designlessons.pdf [accessed February 2007].
Gutbezahl, J.
2007   *NASA space science education/public outreach: Summative evaluation report, March 1998-June 2007.* Prepared for the NASA Science Mission Directorate by Program Evaluation and Research Group at Lesley University. (In collaboration with Susan Baker Cohen, Sabra Lee, and Jodi Sandler.) Available: http://science.hq.nasa.gov/research/NASA_2007_Summative_report.pdf [accessed February 2007].
Hall, G.
2007   *A review of the literature and the INSPIRE model: STEM in out-of-school time.* Paper prepared for the National Research Council Committee to Review and Evaluate NASA's Pre-college Education Program, Washington, DC. Available: http://www.nationalacademies.org/bose/NASA_PreCollege_Eval_Study_Homepage.html [accessed February 2007].
Hernandez, V., McGee, S., Kirby, J., Reese, D., and Martin, J.
2004a   *NASA explorer schools evaluation brief 2. A program in the making: Evidence from summer 2003 workshops.* Report sponsored by NASA (NES/EB2/2-2004) and prepared by Classroom of the Future Center for Educational Technologies®, Erma Ora Byrd Center for Educational Technologies®, Wheeling Jesuit University. Available: http://www.cet.edu/research/pdf/EPHernandez04.pdf [accessed February 2007].
2004b   *NASA explorer schools evaluation brief 3. A program in the making: Year 1 annual report.* Report sponsored by NASA (NES/EB3/7-2004) and prepared by Classroom of the Future Center for Educational Technologies®, Erma Ora Byrd Center for Educational Technologies®, Wheeling Jesuit University. Available: http://www.cet.edu/research/pdf/NES-EB3.pdf [accessed February 2007].

Hidi, S., and Renninger, K.A.
2006   The four-phase model of interest development. *Educational Psychologist, 41*(2), 111-127.
Hopkins, R.
2007a   Implementation plan. *SpaceRef.com Newsletter.* Available: http://www.spaceref.com/news/viewsr.html?pid=24700 [accessed July 2007].
2007b   *Strategic communications framework implementation plan.* Available: http://images.spaceref.com/news/2007/StratCommPlan.2007.06.26.pdf [accessed June 2007].
Horn, J.G., and McKinley, K.H.
2004   *Evaluation of the National Aeronautics and Space Administration aerospace education services program (NASA-AESP).* Technical report submitted to NASA by Evaluation Center, Western Michigan University.
2006   *The final report of a study of the aerospace education service program's role and impact among selected partners.* Report prepared for NASA by Oklahoma State University.
House, E.R.
2006   *Blowback: Consequences of evaluation for evaluation.* Keynote address to the American Evaluation Association, November 4, Portland, OR. University of Colorado professor emeritus.
International Technology Education Association
2000   *Standards for technological literacy: Content for the study of technology.* Reston, VA: Author.
Kerlinger, F.N., and Lee, H.B.
2000   *Foundations of behavioral research: Fourth edition.* Fort Worth, TX: Harcourt College.
Kuhn, D., and Franklin, S.
2006   The second decade: What develops (and how)? In W. Damon and R. Lerner (Series Eds.) and D. Kuhn and R. Siegler (Vol. Eds.), *Handbook of child psychology: Cognition, perception, and language* (vol. 2, 6th ed., pp. 953-993). Hoboken, NJ: Wiley.
Lach, M.
2007   *Federal STEM education programs: Educators' perspectives.* Testimony before the House Subcommittee on Research and Science Education, May 15. Available: http://democrats.science.house.gov/Media/File/Commdocs/hearings/2007/research/15may/lach_testimony.pdf [accessed October 2007].
Lawrenz, F.
2007   *Summary and critique of selected evaluations of NASA educational programs.* Paper prepared for the National Research Council Committee for the Review and Evaluation of NASA's Pre-College Education Program, Washington, DC. Available: http://www.nationalacademies.org/bose/NASA_PreCollege_Eval_Study_Homepage.html [accessed September 2007].
Lipstein, R., and Renninger, K.A.
2006   Putting things into words: The development of 12-15-year-old students' interest for writing. In P. Boscolo and S. Hidi (Eds.), *Motivation and writing: Research and school practice* (pp. 113-140). New York: Kluwer Academic/Plenum.
McGee, S., Hernandez, V., and Kirby, J.
2003   *NASA explorer schools evaluation brief 1: Evaluation framework, evaluating the quality and impact of the NASA explorer schools program.* Report sponsored by NASA (NES/EB1/7-2003) and prepared by Classroom of the Future Center for Educational Technologies®, Erma Ora Byrd Center for Educational Technologies®, Wheeling Jesuit University. Wheeling, WV: Classroom of the Future. Available: http://www.cet.edu/research/pdf/EPMcgee03.pdf [accessed February 2007].

Moiser, C.I.
1947   A critical examination of the concepts of face validity. *Educational and Psychological Measurement, 7*, 191-206.
Mundry, S.
2007   *Alignment of the NASA explorer school model with models for school improvement and reform.* Paper prepared for the National Research Council Committee for the Review and Evaluation of NASA's Pre-College Education Program, Washington, DC. Available: http://www.nationalacademies.org/bose/NASA_PreCollege_Eval_Study_ Homepage.html [accessed April 2007].
National Aeronautics and Space Administration
1993   *NASA's strategic plan for education: A strategy for change, 1993-1998.* (EP-289, Office of Education.) Washington, DC: Author.
1995   *Partners in education: A strategy for integrating education and public outreach into NASA's space science programs.* Washington, DC: Author, Office of Space Science. Available: http://spacescience.nasa.gov/admin/pubs/edu/educont.htm [accessed February 2007].
1996   *Implementing the Office of Space Science (OSS) education/public outreach strategy: A report by the OSS-space science advisory committee education/public outreach task force.* Washington, DC: Author, Office of Space Science. Available: http://spacescience. nasa.gov/admin/pubs/edu/imp_plan.pdf [accessed February 2007].
2003a   *NASA's education enterprise strategy.* Available: http://education.nasa.gov/pdf/ 55377main_32915-Education_508.pdf [accessed February 2007].
2003b   *NASA 2003 strategic plan.* Available: www.nasa.gov/pdf/1968main_strategi.pdf [accessed February 2007].
2003c   *Space science education and public outreach: Inspiring the next generation of explorers.* (NASA Space Science Education and Public Outreach annual report for federal fiscal year 2003.) Report submitted to the Office of Management and Budget, September 24. Washington, DC: Author.
2006a   *NASA education strategic coordination framework: A portfolio approach.* Adopted by the Education Coordinating Committee, February 24. Available: http://education. nasa.gov/pdf/151156main_NASA_Booklet_final_3.pdf [accessed April 2007].
2006b   *Explanatory guide to the NASA science mission directorate education and public outreach evaluation factors.* Available: http://science.hq.nasa.gov/research/SMD_EPO_ Guide_v2.pdf [accessed February 2007].
2006c   *National SEMAA office performance report: 4th quarter, FY-2006. July 1, 2006- September 30, 2006.* Prepared by Paragon TEC Contract No. NAS3-02123, Cleveland, OH.
2007   *NASA organizational chart.* Available: http://www.nasa.gov/centers/hq/pdf/182318main_ NASA_Org_Chart_July-2007.pdf [accessed July 2007].
National Research Council
1994   *NASA's education programs: Defining goals, assessing outcomes.* Washington, DC: National Academy Press.
1995   *National science education standards.* Center for Science, Mathematics, and Engineering Education National Committee on Science Education Standards and Assessment. Washington, DC: National Academy Press.
2006   *America's lab report: Investigations in high school science.* Committee on High School Science Laboratories: Role and Vision, S.R. Singer, M.L. Hilton, and H.A. Schweingruber (Eds.). Board on Science Education, Division of Behavioral and Social Sciences and Education. Washington, DC: The National Academies Press.

2007a *Rising above the gathering storm: Energizing and employing America for a brighter economic future.* Committee on Prospering in the Global Economy of the 21st Century: An Agenda for American Science and Technology. National Academy of Sciences, National Academy of Engineering, and Institute of Medicine. Washington, DC: The National Academies Press.

2007b *Taking science to school: Learning and teaching science in grades K-8.* Committee on Science Learning K-8, R. Duschl, H.A. Schweingruber, and A. Shouse (Eds.). Board on Science Education, Division of Behavioral and Social Sciences and Education. Washington, DC: The National Academies Press.

2007c *Portals to the universe: The NASA astronomy science centers.* Committee on NASA Astronomy Science Centers. Washington, DC: The National Academies Press.

Penuel, W.R., and Means, B.

1999 *Implementation variation and fidelity in an inquiry science program: An analysis of GLOBE data reporting patterns.* (Research through a grant from the National Science Foundation, ESI-9802033.) Prepared by SRI International, Menlo Park, CA.

President's Commission on Moon, Mars, and Beyond

2004 *A journey to inspire, innovate, and discover.* Available: http://www.aura-astronomy. org/nv/Journey%20to%20Inspire%20Innovate%20and%20Discover.pdf [accessed July 2007].

Renninger, K.A.

2000 Individual interest and its implications for understanding intrinsic motivation. In C. Sansone and J.M. Harackiewicz (Eds.), *Intrinsic motivation: Controversies and new directions* (pp. 373-404). San Diego, CA: Academic Press.

Renninger, K.A., and Hidi, S.

2002 Interest and achievement: Developmental issues raised by a case study. In A. Wigfield and J. Eccles (Eds.), *Development of achievement motivation* (pp. 173-195). New York: Academic Press.

Rosenberg, S.L., Heck, D.J., and Banilower, E.R.

2005 *Does teacher content preparation moderate the impacts of professional development? A longitudinal analysis of LSC teacher questionnaire data.* Prepared for the National Science Foundation by Horizon Research, Inc. Available: http://www.pdmathsci.net/ reports/rosenberg_heck_banilower_2005.pdf [accessed February 2007].

Rosendahl, J., Sakimoto, P., Pertzborn, R., and Cooper, L.

2004 The NASA office of space science education and public outreach program. *Advances in Space Research, 24,* 2127-2135.

Rossi, P.H., and Freeman, H.E.

1993 *Evaluation: A systematic approach, fifth edition.* Thousand Oaks, CA: Sage.

Schwerin, T.

2006 *NASA education portfolio: Data call.* Prepared by the Institute for Global Environmental Strategies, conducted under NASA Grant NNG04GE83G (May 31). Available: http:// www.strategies.org/Portfolio/Final/ExecutiveSummaryReport.pdf [accessed June 2007].

Shadish, W., Cook, T., and Campbell, D.

2002 *Experimental and quasi-experimental designs for generalized causal inference.* Boston, MA: Houghton Mifflin.

Supovitz, J.A., and Turner, H.M.

2000 The effects of professional development on science teaching practices and classroom culture. *Journal of Research on Science Teaching, 37,* 963-980.

Tai, R.H., Liu, C.Q., Maltese, A.V., and Fan, X.

2006 Planning early for careers in science. *Science, 312,* 1143-1144. Available: http://www. sciencemag.org/cgi/reprint/312/5777/1143.pdf [accessed October 2007].

Torgerson, D.J., and Roberts, C.
1999   Understanding controlled trials: Baseline imbalance in randomized controlled trials. *British Medical Journal, 319*(7203), 185.
Torgerson, D.J., and Torgerson, C.J.
2003   Avoiding bias in randomized controlled trials in educational research. *British Journal of Educational Studies, 51,* 36-46.
U.S. Department of Education
2006   *10 facts about K-12 education funding.* Available: http://www.ed.gov/about/overview/fed/10facts/index.html [accessed June 2007].
2007a   *Report of the Academic Competitiveness Council.* (May). Available: http://www.ed.gov/about/inits/ed/competitiveness/acc-mathscience/index.html [accessed February 2007].
2007b   *Overview.* Available: http://www.ed.gov/about/landing.jhtml?src=gu [accessed June 2007].
Weiss, C.
1998   *Evaluation: Methods for studying programs and policies.* Upper Saddle River, NJ: Prentice Hall.
Weiss, I.
2007   *Federal STEM education programs: Educators' perspectives. May 15, 2007.* Testimony before the Subcommittee on Research and Science Education of the House Committee on Science and Technology. Available: http://democrats.science.house.gov/Media/File/Commdocs/hearings/2007/research/15may/weiss_testimony.pdf [accessed June 2007].
Westat
2001   *NASA education program evaluation review (NEPER): Final report.* Unpublished paper (August). Rockville, MD: Author.
Westmoreland, H., and Little, P.
2006   *Exploring quality standards for middle school after school programs: What we know and what we need to know. A summit report.* Harvard Family Research Project; Cambridge, MA. Available: www.gse.harvard.edu/hfrp/content/projects/afterschool/conference/summit-2005-summary.pdf [accessed March 2007].
Winterton, J.
2007   *Federal STEM (science, technology, engineering, and mathematics) education programs.* Testimony before the House Subcommittee on Research and Science Education of the Committee on Science and Technology (June 6). Available: http://democrats.science.house.gov/Media/File/Commdocs/hearings/2007/research/06jun/winterton_testimony.pdf [accessed June 2007].

Appendix A

Biographical Sketches of Committee Members and Staff

Helen R. Quinn *(Chair)* is a professor of physics at Stanford University and also serves as education and public outreach manager at the Stanford Linear Accelerator Center. She has published widely and holds numerous honors from scientific organizations. In addition to her scholarly work in theoretical physics, she is also interested in science education and the continuing education of science teachers. She was an active contributor to the California state science curriculum reforms and currently serves as the president of the nonprofit Contemporary Physics Education Project. She is an elected member of the National Academy of Sciences, and she is also a member and past president of the American Physical Society. At the National Research Council, she served as a member of the Committee on Physics of the Universe, and she also served on the Federal Coordinating Committee on Science, Mathematics and Technology Education. She received a Ph.D. in physics from Stanford University.

Edward F. Crawley is a professor and head of the Department of Aeronautics and Astronautics at Massachusetts Institute of Technology and a MacVicar faculty fellow. He is currently serving as a member of the NASA Technology and Commercialization Advisory Committee. His current research interests include the design of spacecraft and space systems, the development of intelligent structures with embedded actuators, sensors and processors, and the architecture of large engineering systems. He was a finalist in the NASA astronaut selection in 1980, is an active pilot, and was the 1990 and 1995 northeast regional soaring champion. He has served as chair of several professional organizations and is currently chairing the Soaring Society of America Structures and Materials Panel. He is an elected member of the National Academy of Engineering and a fellow of the AIAA (American Institute of Aeronautics and Astronautics). He served on the Presidential Advisory Committee on the Space Station Redesign. He received S.B. and S.M. degrees in aeronautics and astronautics and a Sc.D. in structural dynamics from the Massachusetts Institute of Technology.

Michael A. Feder *(Program Officer)* is on the staff of the Board on Science Education. He has a background in child development and education evaluation. At the National Research Council, he is also serving as a program officer for the Committee on Learning Science in Informal Environments and the Committee on Understanding and Improving K-12 Engineering Education. Previously, he worked as an education program evaluator, contributing to such projects as a review of interventions for English-language learners and the evaluation of the Mathematics and Science Partnership Programs in New Jersey and Ohio. His research work included the effects of subsidized non-Head Start day care on the academic achievement of Hispanic children and the psychological and academic adjustment of refugee children exposed to wartime trauma. He has a Ph.D. in applied developmental psychology from George Mason University.

Ernest R. House is emeritus professor in the School of Education at the University of Colorado at Boulder. His primary interests are evaluation and policy analysis. Previously, he was an associate professor at the Center for Instructional Research and Curriculum Evaluation at the University of Illinois, Urbana-Champaign. He is a recipient of the 1989 Harold E. Lasswell Prize presented by *Policy Sciences* and of the 1990 Paul F. Lazarsfeld award for evaluation theory presented by the American Evaluation Association. He has authored numerous books and peer-reviewed articles on evaluation and policy and has served on the editorial board of several professional journals in evaluation. He has been a visiting scholar at the University of California at Los Angeles, Harvard University, and the University of New Mexico, as well as in England, Australia, Spain, Sweden, Austria, and Chile. He has served on several advisory boards and committees, including the Federal Coordinating Committee on Science, Mathematics and Technology Education, and led several evaluations and assessments of science, technology, engineering, and mathematics and other programs. He received a B.A. in English from Washington University, an M.S. in secondary education from Southern Illinois University, and an Ed.D. from the University of Illinois.

Harriett G. Jenkins is a retired member of the federal Senior Executive Service who consults on a variety of projects. Formerly, she served as director of the Office of Senate Fair Employment Practices in the U.S. Senate and as the assistant administrator for Equal Opportunity Programs at NASA, working both with agency staff and with historically black colleges and universities and other minority universities. Prior to her federal career, she served as a teacher, vice principal, principal, director of elementary education, and assistant superintendent for instruction in the Berkeley Unified School District in California. She has received numerous awards, including two President's Meritorious Executive Awards (1980, 1992) and the President's Distinguished Executive Award (1983), as well as several awards from NASA. She is an elected fellow of the National Academy of Public Administration. In 2000, NASA honored her by establishing in her name the "Harriett G. Jenkins Pre-doctoral Fellowship Program." She received a B.A. in mathematics from Fisk, which also awarded her an honorary doctorate of science. She has an M.A. in education and an Ed.D. in policy, planning, and administration, both from the University of California at Berkeley, and a J.D. from Georgetown University.

Brett D. Moulding is director of curriculum and instruction at the Utah State Office of Education. He provides statewide leadership for education policy and programs, including development and implementation of the Utah core curriculum, core assessment, and statewide professional development of K-12 teachers. Previously, he served as president of the Council of State Science Supervisors, and he is currently a member of the steering committee for the revision of the 2009 Science Framework for the National Assessment of Educational Progress. Prior to working at the Utah Office of Education, he was a high school chemistry teacher for 20 years, and in 1992 he received the Presidential Award for Excellence in Mathematics and Science Teaching. Mr. Moulding has an M.S. in education with emphasis on science from Weber State University.

Bruce Partridge is professor of astronomy at Haverford College. His research activities involve the use of radio astronomy to answer questions about the origin and evolution of galaxies and clusters of galaxies, and his related work includes preparation for the Planck Surveyor Satellite, to be launched by the European Space Agency to study the structure of the universe. His role in national and international scientific societies has included strategic planning in physics and astronomy and reform in higher education. He has served as education officer of the American Astronomical Society, an elective post charged with advising on educational policies and practices at all levels. He currently serves on several advisory committees to departments and programs at the California Institute of Technology and the Astronomical Society of the Pacific and as a referee for a number of physics and astronomy journals. He has received many awards and is a member of the American Astronomical Society and the International Astronomical Union. He has an A.B. in physics from Princeton University and a Ph.D. in physics from Oxford University.

Senta Raizen is director of the National Center for Improving Science Education at WestEd. She has been involved in science education for over four decades, starting with her position as a program officer at the National Science Foundation. She has dealt with all aspects of science education, including curriculum improvement, assessment, professional development, program evaluation, and research and policy analysis, including the dissemination and use of research. In her current position, she has led or participated in many projects aimed at science education reform for 2000 and beyond. She has also led several major evaluation efforts, including evaluation of federally sponsored programs that provide preparation and professional development for science and math educators. She has served as advisor to several national and international student assessment programs and to and federal and private agencies. She has a B.S. in chemistry from Guilford College and an M.A. in physical science from Bryn Mawr College.

Philip J. Sakimoto is the professional specialist on outreach and diversity at Notre Dame University with the mission of making science accessible to the broadest possible audience. Previously, he spent 14 years with NASA's education and minority access programs, most recently serving as acting director of NASA's Space Science Education and Public Outreach Program. His contributions include participation in several committees for increasing diversity at NASA and in space science. Dr. Sakimoto was the assistant director for the Johns Hopkins Space Grant Consortium as well as a research scientist and professor at the university. He served as chair of the astronomy department at Whitman College. He has published several NASA technical reports, and has written for scientific journals on space exploration and ultraviolet astronomy. He has lectured internationally on topics in astronomy and diversity in science. Dr. Sakimoto received a B.A. in physics from Pomona College and both an M.A. and a Ph.D. in astronomy from the University of California, Los Angeles.

Heidi A. Schweingruber *(Study Director)* is the acting director of the Board on Science Education. She codirected the National Research Council study that produced *Taking Science to School: Learning and Teaching Science in Grades K-8*, in 2007 and was a program officer on the study that produced *America's Lab Report: Investigations in High School Science*. Prior to joining the National Research Council, she was a program officer for the preschool curriculum evaluation program and for a grant program in mathematics education at the Institute of Education Sciences in the U.S. Department of Education. She was also a liaison to the Department of Education's Mathematics and Science Initiative and an adviser to the Early Reading First Program. Before moving into policy work, she was the director of research for the Rice University School Mathematics Project, an outreach program in K-12 mathematics education, and she taught in the psychology and education departments. She has a Ph.D. in developmental psychology and anthropology and a certificate in culture and cognition from the University of Michigan.

Elizabeth K. Stage is director of Lawrence Hall of Science, the public science center at the University of California at Berkeley. Previously, she directed the Mathematics Professional Development Institutes under the Office of the President of the University of California. Her work has focused on increasing opportunities for all students to learn worthwhile mathematics and science. She is president-elect of the National Center for Science Education, an elected fellow of the American Association for the Advancement of Science, and a former member and chair of the California Curriculum Commission. She serves as an expert in student assessment with the Organisation for Economic Co-operation and Development. She has an Ed.D. in science education and an M.Ed., both from Harvard University, and an A.B. in chemistry from Smith College, which also awarded her the Smith College Medal in 1996.

James S. Trefil is Clarence J. Robinson Professor of Physics at George Mason University. As both a physicist and author, his word concentrates on writing and teaching science to nonscientists. He has served as contributing editor for science for *USA TODAY Weekend,* as a regular contributor and science consultant for *Smithsonian* and *Astronomy* magazines, as a science commentator and member of the Science Advisory Board for National Public Radio and for numerous Public Broadcasting Service productions, and as principal science consultant to the Adler Planetarium in Chicago. He is currently chief science consultant to the McDougal-Littell Middle School Science Project. He held visiting faculty appointments at many U.S. and European universities and laboratories, and he held several appointments as visiting scholar at the Department of Geophysical Sciences at the University of Chicago. He is a fellow of the American Physical Society and a former Guggenheim fellow. He has a B.S. in physics from the University of Illinois, both a B.A. and an M.A. from Oxford University, and both an M.S. and a Ph.D. in theoretical physics from Stanford University.

Carol H. Weiss is professor of education emerita at Harvard Graduate School of Education where she teaches courses on evaluation, organizational decision making, and research methods. Her ongoing research deals with educational policy making, the uses of research in policy making, and the influence of ideology, interests, information, and institutional rules and structures. She has written 11 books and about 100 articles and book chapters dealing with evaluation, uses of research in policy making, cross-national comparisons of research influence, and media reporting of research. Her recent work includes *Evaluation: Methods for Studying Programs and Policies*, *What to Do Until the Random Assigner Comes*, and *The Interface Between Evaluation and Public Policy*, which was published internationally. She has been a fellow at the Center for Advanced Study in Behavioral Sciences, a senior fellow at the U.S. Department of Education, and a guest scholar at the Brookings Institution. She has a B.A. in government from Cornell, an M.A. in government from Columbia, and a Ph.D. in sociology from Columbia University.

Appendix B

Acronyms

ACC	Academic Competitiveness Council
AESP	Aerospace Education Services Project
ARD	Aeronautics Research Directorate
ARISS	Amateur Radio on the International Space Station
DLN	Digital Learning Network
DoC	Department of Commerce
DoED	Department of Education
EAP	Educator Astronaut Project
EFP	Education Flight Projects
EHR	Education and Human Resources Directorate
ESEA	Elementary and Secondary Education Act
ESMD	Exploration Systems Mission Directorate
ESSEA	Earth Systems Science Education Alliance
FCCSET	Federal Coordinating Council for Science, Engineering and Technology
GEMS	Great Explorations in Math and Science
GLOBE	Global Learning and Observation to Benefit the Environment
IDEAS	Initiative to Develop Education through Astronomy and Space Science
IES	Institute of Education Sciences

INSPIRE	Interdisciplinary National Science Project Incorporating Research and Education Experience
MUREP	Minority University Research and Education Program
NAEP	National Assessment of Educational Progress
NASA	National Aeronautics and Space Administration
NASSMC	National Alliance of State Science and Mathematics Coalitions
NCEE	National Center for Education Evaluation
NCER	National Center for Education Research
NCES	National Center for Education Statistics
NCLB	No Child Left Behind
NCSER	National Center for Special Education Research
NEAT	Network of Educator Astronaut Teachers
NEEIS	NASA Education Evaluation Information System
NES	NASA Explorer Schools
NSF	National Science Foundation
NSTA	National Science Teachers Association
OES	Office of Earth Science
OSS	Office of Space Science
REL	Regional Education Lab
SEMAA	Science, Engineering, Mathematics and Aerospace Academy
SMD	Science Mission Directorate
SOMD	Space Operations Mission Directorate
STEM	Science, technology, engineering, and mathematics
STEM-G	Science, technology, engineering, mathematics, and geography
TERC	Began 40 years ago as Technical Education Research Centers, now simply known as TERC